—— MAINE —— LOBSTERBOATS

MAINE LOBSTERBOATS

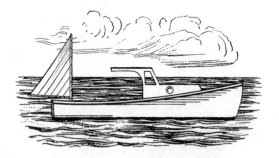

Builders and Lobstermen
Speak of Their Craft

by
Virginia L. Thorndike

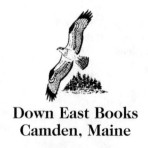

Down East Books
Camden, Maine

Text copyright © 1998 by Virginia L. Thorndike
ISBN 0-89272-403-X

Printed and bound at BookCrafters, Inc.

9   8   7   6   5   4   3   2

Down East Books
P.O. Box 679
Camden, Maine 04843
BOOK ORDERS: 1-800-766-1670

Library of Congress Cataloging-in-Publication Data

Thorndike, Virginia L.
    Maine lobsterboats: builders and lobstermen speak of their craft / by
Virginia L. Thorndike.
        p.   cm.
    ISBN 0-89272-403-X (pbk.)
    1. Fishing boats—Maine—Design and construction. 2. Lobster
fisheries—Maine. 3. Lobster fishers—Maine—Interviews.
4. Boatbuilders—Maine—Interviews. I. Title.
VM431.T49 1998
623.8'231—dc21   98-3275
                                                   CIP

CONTENTS

PREFACE

Maine lobsterboats symbolize the coast of Maine—not just at home, but away as well. They are vehicles for lobster fishermen, of course, and were developed for that purpose, but they fulfill many other functions now because of their sheer usefulness. A recent magazine photograph showed a clutch of them in a marina, where they were serving their Chesapeake Bay owners as pleasure boats. They carry kayakers to campsites; they fish for urchins and tend salmon pens; they act as trucks, taxicabs, tourist buses, and rescue vessels.

I was brought up with a pleasure boat built on a lobsterboat hull. Nowadays, some would call her a "lobster yacht." (Others are horrified by the expression and prefer the term "down east cruiser.") Her name was *Questor,* and she was built in 1957 of cedar planks on oak frames by Newbert and Wallace in Thomaston, Maine. She could take whatever came her way, and she was beautiful. I thought so at the time and grew up accepting her lines as the standard against which all boats should be measured. She was a no-nonsense pleasure boat, whose mahogany trim was present but limited, and she was laid out to be comfortable. Her heavy, full-displacement hull was happy at ten knots.

She summered in Islesboro's Seal Harbor while we owned her. Then, in 1964, my parents sold her to our neighbors, who changed her name to *Owl,* moved her a half-mile southwest (to the entrance of Seal Harbor), and let their caretaker, Wentworth Durkee, watch over her for them. She remains in the Moseley family, although the younger generation has sold the big house and established itself on a small island off the point. The boat is still called *Owl,* and she rests on a mooring a half-mile east across the same cove, from which she serves as transport to the island. She remains under the care of Went Durkee, and although I think of her even now as *Questor,* I recognize Went as her person. He has been with her nearly thirty years, compared to our eight. I still think she's beautiful.

Soon after moving back to Maine, my husband, Phil, and I purchased our own lobsterboat-based vessel. Much as we admired wood, our finances and personal temperaments were far better suited to a material that would require less maintenance; *Sea Smoke* is fiberglass. She is a little shorter than *Questor*—

thirty-two feet to *Questor*'s thirty-six—though probably just as wide. *Sea Smoke* is a modern, "semi-planing" boat—much lighter and faster than *Questor*, but perhaps not always as comfortable. Most important, however, she was put together with the same goals of simplicity and functionality, with the same sense of aesthetic rightness.

Sea Smoke has taken us into many different harbors along the Maine coast, and in each, we looked at the local lobsterboats until we developed an eye not only for what we liked more and what we liked less, but also for the different philosophies and techniques of the designers and builders who created these boats. Writing this book gave us the excuse to seek out these people and to talk with them about their work, as well as the fishermen and others who have used Maine lobsterboats for such a great variety of tasks.

I hope I offend no one by what's included or not included, or by the manner in which I represent anybody. I simply didn't have time to speak with all the people whose names were suggested to me, and any omissions should not be taken as meaningful, but rather, happenstance. Nor does the inclusion of one builder instead of another imply any sort of endorsement. The Maine coast is home to many builders of high-quality boats—in addition, perhaps, to one or two builders of less-than-high-quality boats—and I couldn't cover all of them. I also have made no attempt whatsoever to discuss Nova Scotia-built lobsterboats, although there are a great number of those on the coast here. And certainly every Maine harbor has its master storytellers—I wish we could have talked with every one of them.

I shall have to make do with thanking all of the people who did speak with me. This book is their story as much as that of the boats. Particular thanks have to go to Avery Kelley, upon whom I called a number of times for one thing or another, and to the Hollands, particularly Glenn. He not only built *Sea Smoke* some ten years before we met him and her, but also provided a great deal of information on a number of subjects. Admittedly, not all of it could be printed. Steve and Lynn Wessel, Mac Pettegrow, Willis Beal, and the late Carroll Lowell were of continuing help, too.

I also would like to thank Sam Manning for his fine drawings, which show construction and design details more clearly than could photographs, and for his thoughtful consideration of the glossary. I feel fortunate to include among my friends such resources as Sam and Susan Manning.

People who have graciously allowed me to use their photographs include Carroll Lowell, Trudy Porter, Brian Robbins, Jim Rockefeller, and Steve and Lynn Wessel. I also appreciate the cooperativeness of the *Waldo County Independent*. And, this book is a lot better than it would otherwise have been due to the efforts of editor Chris Cornell. Thank you all.

As ever, I thank my husband, Phil Roberts, a better partner than whom I cannot imagine.

"It's like buying a penny grab bag. Every time you haul a trap, you might have five lobsters, you might not have one. Every trap is a surprise. And you only get what you put into it. You keep your equipment good and your boat good, and you feel like a millionaire."

—Bobby Lowberg, Rockport

INTRODUCTION
The Maine Lobsterboat and How She Got That Way

What is a lobsterboat? The easy answer is that it's a boat used for lobstering, but the Maine lobsterboat is a recognizable type, whether it's lobstering or not. Lobsterboats are used for many jobs, and those who produce them make as much or more money building pleasure boats, research vessels, and boats for other fisheries as they do turning out lobsterboats.

To her people, a lobsterboat may be simply a tool, but in far more cases, she is a worthy being, deserving of respect and affection. And lobsterboat people have an interest in each other, too. They aren't necessarily all friends—hardly that—but everyone involved in the world of lobsterboats shares something they all recognize as important. Every boat has a designer, a builder, possibly a separate finisher, and an owner, and each of these people plays a role in making her the boat she is. In earlier days, a single person often acted in most of these roles, giving each vessel their own stamp. Today, however, fiberglass has proliferated boats that are identical in hull form, if nothing else, and has made specialization of task the differentiating factor.

But lobsterboat people are still all lobsterboat people.

Designer Spencer Lincoln enjoys planning a working vessel that does its job for its owners and does that job well, and he recognizes the suitability of some of those vessels as pleasure boats. Builder Mac Pettegrow knows the handling characteristics and aesthetics of dozens—scores—of different models of

1

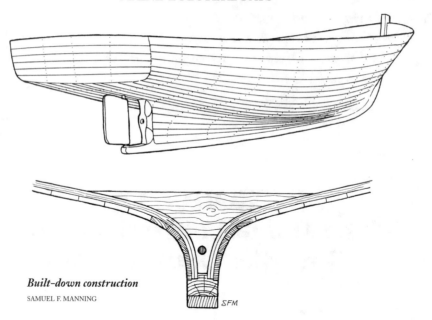

Built-down construction
SAMUEL F. MANNING

lobsterboats, just because he enjoys knowing. Designer/builder/fisherman Willis Beal has lived through the major transition of the Maine lobsterboat from a narrow, elegant wooden hull to a big, boxy fiberglass one, and he admires each type for its respective value.

Fisherman Gweeka Williams wants a useful lobsterboat—he makes his living hauling traps—but he wants her beautiful, and he wants her fast, because he loves to race. And he'll take care of his boat like the aristocrat she is. Avery Kelley has purse-seined in his big fiberglass lobsterboat, and he admires her capabilities a great deal. But the pride and affection he feels for his little classic wooden lobsterboat *Bookie B* are similar to what people feel for their dogs or even family members.

Normally measuring from twenty to fifty feet in length, the modern Maine lobsterboat is nearly always a single-engined vessel, one with a distinctive arrangement of house and cockpit. Forward, she has a low trunk cabin, which provides at least minimal accommodation and, on smaller working lobsterboats, space for the gas or diesel inboard engine. Aft of the trunk cabin, usually about amidships, her standing shelter—complete with windshield and canopy top—provides cover for the helmsman. The standing shelter, or house, may be enclosed on three sides, left open to the elements, or fitted with removable panels on a seasonal basis to provide additional protection. The open cockpit runs from the after edge of the standing shelter to the stern. On a working lobsterboat, this cockpit may be half the length of the boat; on a heav-

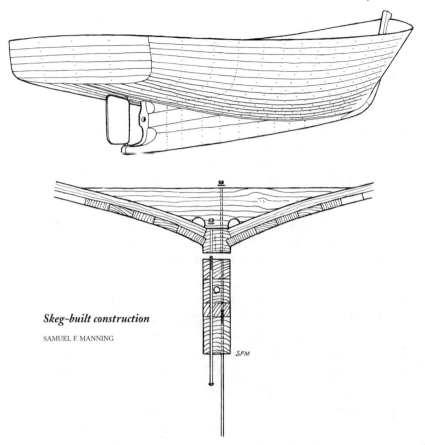

Skeg-built construction

SAMUEL F. MANNING

ily dressed pleasure boat with an extended house, it may be far smaller.

A Maine lobsterboat is recognizable wherever she goes because of her proportions, shape, and layout. Particularly distinctive is the graceful upward curve of the rails, starting low in the stern and rising to the bow. The late Carroll Lowell, born and bred to be a designer and builder of lobsterboats, captures the essence of the classic look: "The sheer gives them away. Low freeboard, the sheer, and the long, sleek waterline." Chesapeake workboats share some of the features of the Maine lobsterboat, including the short distance from water to rail (freeboard), but their standing shelters are smaller and placed farther forward, making them look awkward to a person who has grown up around Maine boats.

Beneath the water, the lobsterboat hull features a sharp V forward, at the bow, and is relatively flat aft, at the stern. Among Maine lobsterboats, there are two principal hull configurations: built-down and skeg-built. The built-down boats developed from Friendship sloops and other early sailing vessels, the keel shrinking as the sail disappeared. The construction, however, remained the same, with graceful double-curved ribs providing a smooth transition from bilge to keel.

By contrast, the skeg-built boat is designed with an external keel—like a skeg on a skiff or a fin keel on a sailboat. The skeg boat is less expensive to build in wood and tends to be lighter and faster, while some say the built-down boat is stronger and more kindly in a sea. Both configurations are now widely produced in fiberglass. There are proponents of each style, few of whom would consider building or owning a boat of the other type.

Perhaps the clearest distinction between a Maine lobsterboat hull and any other type is the way it reacts to power. A full-displacement boat, like a traditional sailboat, pushes through the water and will only go so fast, regardless of how much power is applied. When she's driven faster than she likes, she'll pull herself down into the water or, at least, leave a horrendous wake behind her. At the other end of the design spectrum, a modern planing powerboat with a deep-V hull is designed to climb up on top of the water and is very efficient when she gets there. At lower speeds, however, such a boat is clumsy, hard to handle, and fuel-thirsty.

The Maine lobsterboat has a semi-displacement—or semi-planing—hull. As Spencer Lincoln says with reverence, "The absolutely lovely characteristic of a lobsterboat is the relationship between boat speed and engine rpm. For each application of the throttle, you get a commensurate increase in speed."

There are people who get mystical about Maine lobsterboats. Dick Pulsifer, who builds elegant pleasure boats on an early lobsterboat model called the Hampton boat, describes one: "It's how she keeps the water; it's what you see and what you don't see. The sex appeal of a lobster yacht is it's so breathtaking—it says so much about the people that buy it. These boats just do what they're supposed to do.

"So much is in the eye of the builder, hopefully unhampered by the architect or the owner. It's the sheer, it's the flare, it's all sorts of shapes, when all sorts of things are just right."

From the beginning, the lobsterboat was developed for her job. The improvements and changes over the years have always been in response to a new technology or a new demand from lobster fishermen. In the early days, the typical Maine lobsterman worked fifty to a hundred wooden traps, and he fished from a peapod, powered by oars, or a Friendship sloop, driven by sails. "The gasoline engine came along and changed the whole thing," says veteran lobsterboat builder Mac Pettegrow of Southwest Harbor. "But even after fishermen went to power, a lot of their boats were converted sloops, with the masts taken out."

The typical early gasoline engine weighed a hundred pounds per horsepower, and fishermen soon realized that they needed a larger, wider hull to sup-

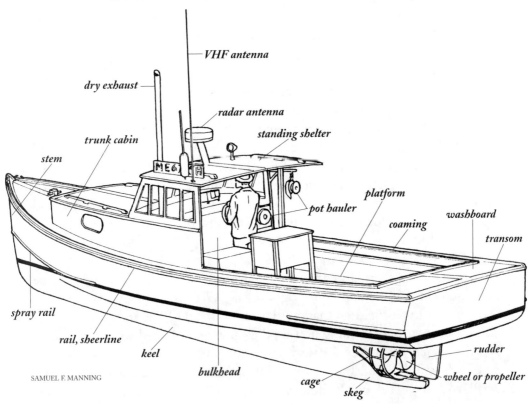

VHF antenna
dry exhaust
radar antenna
trunk cabin
standing shelter
stem
platform
pot hauler
washboard
coaming
transom
spray rail
rail, sheerline
keel
bulkhead
cage
skeg
rudder
wheel or propeller

SAMUEL F. MANNING

port the extra weight. At the same time, the engine permitted a bigger, heavier vessel, as the fisherman no longer had to be able to row his boat when the wind let him down.

Then came Will Frost of Beals Island. "He's the guy who built the down east lobsterboat," says Mac. "He was the first to build a skeg-style boat. Before Will Frost, all lobsterboats were deep, bulky hand-me-downs from displacement boats like the Friendship sloops. Will was the first guy who took a rowing skiff and enlarged it and had something that would move decently with a gasoline engine in it."

"Once they'd launched one," he continues, "it wasn't long before they took the straight-eight Buick engine out of Mother's Roadmaster and saw that the boat could go twenty knots. That's when they started playing with all these different things to make them go even faster." The primary change and the feature that typifies the skeg-built Maine lobsterboat even today is its straight run—the straight path water takes as it travels beneath the boat—and that started with Will Frost after World War I.

Whether Frost was single-handedly responsible for all the changes or not, there is no question that something major had happened in Jonesport. And so it was that nearby Beals Island, part of Jonesport until 1925, became a major center of lobsterboat building.

All the early boats were long, narrow, and open, with (at most) a low canvas shelter forward. The engine was in the hauling area, covered by a box, and the fisherman was out in the weather all the time. The first change to the layout was the addition of a trunk cabin. Some lobstermen then built a little open-backed box onto the trunk cabin and stood under it when they were at the wheel, but they were still hauling out in the open.

Willis Beal has been a fisherman since he was a boy, and he was the last man building wooden lobsterboats on Beals Island. Willis says his father had the first true standing shelter, or hauling house, in their area. That was in the early '40s. "He was having Harold Gower build him a boat, and he'd seen pleasure boats with houses down around Mount Desert Island. He thought it would work real well on a lobsterboat," says Willis, "so he drew it out for Harold, and Harold built it."

The lobsterboat with the standing shelter seemed a strange sight; Willis reports that one fisherman said if it was his boat, the first thing he'd do is take an ax and cut that hauling house right off it. "Well," said Willis's father, "if it was your boat you could do that, but it's my boat, and I like it." By the 1950s, all the new boats had hauling houses, the cabin was isolated with a bulkhead, and the engine was moved forward, so that half of it was in the house and half was in the trunk cabin. Like many, Willis's father's boat had side seats and a small coal stove below. "Fishing winters, you had some heat," remembers Willis. We camped right in it when we tended weirs out at Roque Island. And don't things taste good when they're cooked in a boat!"

Arno Day is a well-respected builder from Sedgwick. He says that the rush to speed wasn't universal and that most of the boats built after World War II were like those of before the war. "We were still using small engines, those Gray Marine engines. We'd put a twenty-five-horse engine in a twenty-eight-footer, and it made a good little boat to work around the shore." In his area, that boat had a displacement hull, "with a design such that it went very easily through the water," says Arno. "A fisherman would have a hundred and fifty traps, and as he fished around the shore, he could move the traps as fast as the lobsters moved.

"After the war, when the boys came home, the lobsters had been resting awhile, so there was a good supply," says Arno. "Little by little, the fishermen got greedier and greedier, and they went to bigger and bigger engines, and bigger and bigger boats. Now, they're fishing a thirty-eight-foot boat and twelve hundred traps."

"It was hydraulics that made a big change in lobsterboats," said Carroll Lowell. "When hydraulic pot haulers came in, in 1963 or '64, I never thought they'd sell, but it didn't take long for them to catch on. Today, the fisherman's not using his back over a capstan—up the traps come, and they stop when they get there."

Willis Beal never questioned that the pot hauler would catch on. "Men's arms and shoulders were playing out, pulling on those hoisters. With the manual steering and hoisting, at noontime I couldn't turn my head but one way, and only just so far. It ached so bad when I got home, I could hardly eat. Man after man was having bursitis, different things in their shoulders, and it's a known fact that fishermen have trouble with their backs anyway 'cause they work more on one side than the other."

Willis gives credit to nylon for increasing the number of traps one man could handle. Before nylon, the netting tunnels inside the trap, called the "heads," had to be replaced twice a year, and the line running from the trap to the buoy, called the "warp" was inherently weak. "A man could only handle about two hundred traps and keep them in shape," says Willis. "And with rope

The early engine-powered lobsterboats were open except for a canvas shelter forward.

that could only support two traps, you were limited. With nylon, you could put traps out for a longer time, and you could put more than two traps on a warp—you didn't have to worry about it parting."

Then traps constructed of vinyl-coated, welded wire arrived in the early 1980s, and with wood borers no longer a threat, the gear could remain in the water longer still. "If you can have a three-day set," says Willis, "you're better off. The larger the lobsters, the slower they crawl." He explains that in good weather, the lobsterman wants to work every day, and—thanks to today's boats and equipment—he can haul and reset four hundred traps each trip. If he leaves those to soak for the recommended interval, he can pull a second series of four hundred traps the following day, and a third series of four hundred the day after that. "That's the reason they fish twelve hundred traps," says Willis. "It doesn't do any more than keep them busy."

With the introduction and refinement of the pot hauler and then the changes in the materials used in his gear, the typical Maine fisherman wanted a bigger boat to carry all the traps he could now fish. He also wanted a bigger engine to push his bigger boat faster over the greater expanses of water his traps now covered. "Bigger engines found their way into the lobster industry mostly from trucks," Willis says.

"As builders and fishermen went to bigger and bigger engines, the style of boat changed to handle them and go faster," explains Arno. "Every lobsterboat designed in the last fifteen years was designed to win the race on the Fourth of July. The sad part," he says, "is that in going after speed, they've bypassed all the good features that made good workboats. The displacement hulls moved easy, turned easy, and were very seaworthy. The modern ones bounce around and bang and slam and push water around." He smiles quietly. " 'Course I may be a little opinionated, having started so many years ago."

Many people feel the new boats aren't as beautiful as the old ones. Mac Pettegrow says, "They're seagoing pickup trucks—all function, designed to fish a thousand or fifteen hundred traps." He explains that although they must carry huge loads, these boats still have to fish "tight to the shore," so they can't be sixty feet long—they wouldn't be maneuverable enough. Instead, they are beamy and high sided. "They're not such great sea boats any more," says Mac, "and they're not as fast for a given amount of horsepower. But," he adds, "they'll lug tremendous loads of gear, and you can tow a drag for scallops or quahogs, or a big trawl for groundfish. A boat with only an eight-foot beam would be a danger doing that.

"The design now meets the function," Mac explains. "It's just not the pretty boat the rusticators liked, with a pretty sheerline and no fuss in the water. These newer boats have no sheerlines, and they do make a fuss in the water, but they're a safe platform to work out of."

Willis Beal has finally allowed one of his designs to be built in fiberglass. The model being built by RP Boat Shop of Steuben is a good example of the new-style Maine lobsterboat. It measures thirty-five feet long; thirteen feet, six inches wide in the middle; and twelve feet, seven inches wide at the transom. Willis himself admits, "I don't like the looks of it so well, but with the straight sheer, you can get the [cockpit] floor up higher, so it's easier to get up on deck and you can see over the bow better. We're all coming to it down east."

All of the people whose lives revolve around lobsterboats look up as an unfamiliar one appears in their harbor. They give her careful scrutiny, analyzing her, guessing who designed her, who built her, who's working her, and judging how good a job each has done. That's just part of being a lobsterboat person.

In the following pages, you're going to hear the voices of some of these people as they talk about lobstering and the Maine lobsterboat in her various roles. Some reminisce about days and boats gone by. Others talk about work that is going on today and is still evolving. Together, they tell the remarkable story of the Maine lobsterboat.

"If you get 'em you get 'em, if you don't, you don't—
you just do what you can."

—overheard on the VHF radio

LEROY DODGE,
Rockport

"Lobsterboats? I've helped build 'em and rebuild 'em, I've fished 'em, I've damn near sunk a couple of 'em."

Leroy is the harbormaster in Rockport now. He sits in a smoky office on the waterfront, feet up on his desk, his VHF radio squawking from time to time. "I've seen boats sunk, up on their sides, up on the rocks, rope in the wheel—I've seen it all. I have seven brothers and two sisters, and most of them fish. I started fishin' myself when I was in fifth or sixth grade. My father built me a ten-foot skiff with a three-horse outboard on it, and I had anywhere from twenty-five to seventy-five traps. I fished nights, after school, weekends. Back then you could fish Sundays—they didn't have all the crazy laws you got today.

"Fishin' lobsters is a hard life, but a good life. People come down in the summer and see you comin' in with a good haul, and they think it's pretty easy. But there's a lot more work to it than anybody sees. They don't see all the hours you spend at home fixin' traps and paintin' buoys and when your motor goes down and all that. And you go out and find fifty or seventy-five of your traps lost or cut off, you get kinda ugly pretty quick. People don't see the seals out there botherin' everything—they steal a lot of bait, seals do.

"I was talkin' to a couple of fishermen down the coast, and they thought they were being hauled [robbed]. They kept finding [their trap] doors open. But they found a couple of seals was workin' together, pullin' that bungee cord, and openin' them doors. You can generally tell you're bein' bothered by seals: there's big holes in the bait bags and whole fish are missing.

"But one thing all lobster fishermen hate is sailboats. A sailboat'll pick up a buoy with the front of its keel and drag the trap along. Then when it lets go, the trap's over its head so they can't find it again.

"To set a trap up and get it overboard runs you about fifty dollars. But when the boys get fightin' and feudin', they'll cut off two hundred traps and not think a thing about it. Rockport's always been that type of a harbor—they fight like cats and dogs among themselves. There's always been that tradition, no one knows why. It was that way in my father's time and my grandfather's before him. Even when they was herring fishin', they fought one another.

Leroy Dodge

"It's almost impossible to catch them when they're cuttin' traps—but when they figure out who's doin' it, they take care of it themselves. Sometimes it gets right out of hand, and then the state sends down a warden to make sure they don't start gettin' their guns out. Then they all set down and work it out.

"But if someone's in trouble—on the rocks or his boat's broke down—they work together. Doesn't matter if you're madder 'n hell at someone—if he's in trouble, you help him out. It's like families—they're always fightin', but let something happen to one of them, everyone gets together.

"It's a code they have. Like, if they need somethin' they take it, even if it's on your boat. And they expect you'd do the same. A bushel of bait, say. You come down to your boat, and there's a bushel of bait missing. You get on the radio and say you're missing bait, and someone will tell you that he took it, that he was going to replace it this afternoon. Then someone else will come on saying that he's got a bushel, come and get it."

Leroy says he's nearly gone overboard while lobstering. "Once I was fishin' off the Graves in Camden with my brother. I was goin' through a divorce at the time, and I was kinda depressed. I remember tellin' God that I wanted to die." That day, the brothers were fishing doubles, two traps on one warp. "I'd just thrown the second one overboard, and my brother had kicked the boat into gear. The warp took a half hitch around my foot. Well, I grabbed the backboard on the cabin, and I held on as hard as I could, and I hollered at my brother. But that boat just had a straight [exhaust] stack, no muffler, so he didn't hear me. I was being split in two.

"One by one, my fingers let go, and then I went down and hit the floor, smack, face first. I dove underneath the washboard in the stern—I knew I was going overboard. My leg ripped out from underneath the stern, and I asked God not to take me. Right then my brother turned around and seen what was happening. He and I between us pulled enough slack to get me free. My foot swelled up the size of a football, but I was OK. It was God's way of telling me, 'Yes, you still want to live.'"

Lobstering is a dangerous business, all right. But, says Leroy, "Lobster fishin's kind of like bein' an alcoholic: You can go away from it, but you end up right back at it."

"My stepfather, Phil Raynes, was the dean of lobstermen in Camden. He had no compass but could find his way around without one. One day he was out hauling traps in the fog around Sherman's Point, and there was a big yacht near him. He hailed it down. 'What's your problem?' they asked him.

" 'Well, I haven't got one, but you might. You got wheels on that craft?'

" 'No, why?'

" 'Well, you're heading for shore.' He'd nearly finished hauling, so he told them that if they'd wait while he hauled three more traps, he'd lead them in.

"They fell in behind him, and in a little while they noticed he had no compass. 'Where's your compass?' they asked.

" 'Oh, I had one, twenty-five years ago, but I didn't like it, so I threw it overboard.'

—Captain Gilbert Hall, Penobscot Bay Pilot

GEORGE ALLEN
Remembers the Old Days

"Lobster fishermen are a different breed," says Brooklin's George Allen. "They haven't changed too much over the fifty or sixty years that I've known them. A neighbor—Charley Henderson—was a fisherman back when I was a kid, and to hear him, he never caught more than three lobsters in his life. The fishermen were just about the same's they are now; they're all crying, you know. They all say, 'Oh my gosh, lobsters are terrible.'

"We used to have a lot of fun with Charley Henderson. I had two brothers older'n me—I'd be tagging along, but it was all their ideas. Before the Jonesporter, Charley had an old one-lunger; she was about a twenty-three-foot boat. My brother went down there, took the spark plug out, poured a pint of varnish in the cylinder, then went down and watched Charley try to get her going. Well, he couldn't do it. So they said they'd go to the drugstore, get some ether. They poured that ether in and put the plug back in. Well, she started on

15

that, cleaned herself right out. I think they thought they'd blow the head off it. It's a wonder they didn't.

"With that engine, Charley could be down to Tinker's Island and run out of gas, and borrow a coffee can of gas and get home. If you'd give them things half a chance, they'd run.

"After the war, Charley Henderson was old, and he'd had a heart attack. He couldn't go fishin' alone. He came over and he pleaded with me to go with him, but I wa'n't in any position to gamble, and I couldn't see taking the summer off and losing my shirt. 'Oh,' he said, 'I guarantee you'll make a good living,' but he'd spent so much time convincing me that he was starving to death, I didn't go. I will admit that he put all three of his kids through college during the Depression, no problem at all.

"You go down and look at some of these fishermen who are crying right now. They've got radar and everything you can think of—usually a nice new four-wheel-drive pickup and a snowmobile and a four-wheeler, too. They're trying to get rid of some of the profit that they did declare—not to mention what they didn't. I mean, you go down and buy fifty dollars of lobsters from them, they're not running into the house saying, 'Gee, I got to write this down.' I'm not saying they're all this way—but it's probably true. And I got to admit, lobster fishermen as a whole—I'm not talking any one in particular—they're, well, greedy. They'd almost cut their son's traps, if he wanted to go lobstering, just because it was someone new. If I wanted to go lobstering, I'd want to be prepared to lose a lot of gear this year, and everybody knows that. They're not doing it because it's going to hurt their profit—they want the whole of it, that's my feeling.

"But there's a glut of lobsters right now. It's nothing the fishermen have done or the environmentalists or anybody else." George explains his theory that the once-plentiful codfish ate young lobsters, and now that those fish are gone, victims of overfishing, more of the small crustaceans survive. One hears a great many explanations about the numbers of lobsters, but George's is unusual. "That's only my theory," he says. "It may be a cycle, the temperature of the water, and so forth. There's a lot they don't know about lobsters.

"With the wire traps and the high-speed boats and the pot haulers, they can overhandle a heck of a lot of traps, yet the price has stayed up. Back in Charley Henderson's day, sixty or sixty-five was a gang of traps. They'd go out at two, three in the morning, be home by noon, and go do their farming, haying, whatever other things they had to do.

"Boats now are fifteen, sixteen feet wide and forty feet long. Some of them even got microwaves in them. I think somebody said a lobster boat, ready to fish with the engine and that stuff, not the electronics—those can set you back $30,000—costs $95,000. And that's for the cheapest one. Then, at $50 a trap, you'd have to put in a pretty big mortgage—or have enough money so you wouldn't want to go lobstering. But some guys are still lobstering with outboard motors.

"When I was on the schooner *Stephen Taber,* this was in '61 or '62, we come into Vinalhaven, and there was quite an elderly fisherman there. He probably was in his seventies then, maybe higher. He had a dory with a sail, and he sailed right into the float there, where they was selling. He had a five-gallon pail, full of lobsters. I remember Cy Cousins, owned the *Taber,* said to him, 'That's a pretty cheap way to go,' and the fisherman said, 'Yessir, and as long as gas is $1.75 for five gallons, that's the way I'm gonna do it.' Even today, that five gallons of lobsters would give a pretty good day's pay."

"Right up there by Smith's, you got one hung down there, just thought you'd like to know."

"Oh yeah, thanks. 'Preciate it. What's up?"

"Not much, just pushin' water and dodgin' bullets."

—VHF radio conversation

From Lobsters to Liquor

Everyone seems to agree that Prohibition contributed greatly to the economy of down east Maine, and a great number of lobsterboats worked in the smuggling business. "Rum running was common among fishermen along the Maine coast during the Depression," says Ralph Stanley of Southwest Harbor. "A lot of fishermen were in it.

"There was a fellow here in town wanted some alcohol," Ralph recalls. "Another man had a Jonesport boat that made an awful racket—her exhaust went straight in the air, and you could hear that boat wherever it went. He told the fellow, 'I'm making a run, I'll bring you in some alcohol. You be out by the Western Way channel buoy, and when we come by we'll throw you a can.' The buyer couldn't imagine how that boat could come in without being heard, but he went out by the buoy.

"It was a foggy night, and he didn't hear a thing. There wasn't a sound anywhere. He was about ready to give up and go back in, when *swish*, that Jonesporter came along, and the guy handed over a five-gallon can of alcohol as he went by. Never heard a sound, just *swish*. He had an underwater exhaust he could switch onto." The noisy exhaust was just camouflage.

Harold Bunker, who now lives in Owls Head, was born in 1906 and has personal memories of rum-running when he was a boy. His father had leased Wooden Ball Island, out beyond Matinicus, and lobstered there. "We went ashore on the Wooden Ball one spring and picked up four five-gallon cans of alcohol," recalls Harold. "One had water in it, but the other three was all right.

"Then one time a feller out there lobsterin' from Matinicus come up on

19

the low place where we used to land, and we went out to see what he wanted. He had sixteen kegs of rum on deck, and he wanted to know if we'd hide it for him. I rowed it ashore and put it down in the cracks in the rocks. When it come cold, those kegs froze right down there, but he come and got them a couple kegs at a time." Harold says that the sheriff knew the fellow was bringing rum in but couldn't catch him. "He'd put it in his bait barrel, cover it all over with bait, and come up right past the sheriff. He never suspected a thing.

"I went off back of Wooden Ball twenty miles with my father one night, and we went up alongside this big Lunenburg fisherman—the *Carrie Hertel* was her name. She had whiskey piled up that high on the deck [Harold holds his hand three and a half feet off the floor] and of course below, too. My father had been shipmates with the skipper out of Gloucester. They went below, and there was an earthenware jug, and they got drinkin' and drinkin'. I think it was Geneva Gin and I forget what else—Scotch whiskey. I think my father got fifteen or sixteen cases of it. When we got back, he was cagged out, he'd drunk so much. I went ashore to get his housekeeper to drag him home.

"We packed it all in crocus bags [grain bags] and let the boxes go. The next day, we took the stuff and found a place along the shore on Wooden Ball where there was a regular cave you could crawl in. We hid it there. Next day or the day after, two or three sheriffs come out and searched the island, but they couldn't find nothin'."

"This area was almost the headquarters of rum running," says Brooklin resident George Allen. "They used to land it here on the back shore. On a foggy night, they'd load up the lobsterboat, make a couple of trips, and bury it in a brush pile or whatnot. Then someone would come and pick it up and take it wherever they was going." Sometimes, however, such plans backfired.

"Henry Smith cut some wood down on the Flye Point road, and he had a brush pile," recalls George. "The town said, 'You gotta burn that brush, it's too close to the road.' So he started a fire, but somebody'd filled that pile full of alcohol. When the first of the cans started popping, everybody came running and grabbed a three-gallon can and ran off with it. Later, when the revenue fellows asked him about it, he said he just saw people running off, cans under their arms. He never saw anyone's faces.

"You've heard the expression, 'the Real McCoy'?" asks George. "A lot of people don't know that was from the run-running days. A guy bought some of the old Gloucester fishing schooners, and he was carrying some kind of freight. Then the Depression hit, and he got the idea of picking up rum and bringing it here to Maine. He'd lay three miles offshore—back then, that was the territorial limit, so no one could bother him—and lobsterboats would go out and pick up the liquor. That man's name was McCoy, and he was a pretty good guy to do business with, so he was called 'the Real McCoy'."

"A fisherman who happened to get caught would spend a few months in

SAMUEL F. MANNING

A torpedo-stern lobsterboat loads illegal rum from a schooner under cover of darkness.

the jug," says Brooklin's Arno Day. "It would put him out of business for a while. People weren't that concerned about it. There's always a few rummies around, and only a small percentage of that liquor stayed in the Brooklin area."

Arno's mother was the local telephone operator back then. "The ring-leader called her up one time and said, 'If you should happen to hear anything you think we should know, we'd appreciate you letting us in on it. We'll make it worth your while.' But the law caught up with them. They had a big radio-detector, and they found the radio in Brooklin. The revenue cutter *Kickapoo* laid off Brooklin nearly a month and got most of the people involved."

The government's attempts to control the smuggling were rarely that successful. This story, told by George Allen, is typical: "There was a fairly good-size boat, some kind of a distributor. The revenue people come after her, and the only way the boys could beat them was to drop the alcohol overboard and lighten up the boat. The bay was full of alcohol, and it was drifting all over the place. So the lobster fishermen, every one of them, quit lobstering and went to picking up three-gallon cans of alcohol. There was so much, everyone had some, and they couldn't give it away.

"Another time, one of the guys was caught on the back shore here. He was in the *Cinderella,* and she was a pretty fast boat. She was loaded with rum, and they heard the revenue cutter was coming. So they cut their anchor and took off. They were pretty familiar with the area and 'twas high water, so when they come to the lighthouse down here at the end of Naskeag—Blue Hill Light— they come in over the bar, and the revenue cutter had to go around. They lost the agents, but the revenue people shot at the *Cinderella;* there was bullet holes in the stern of her. They beached her out down at Center Harbor, and everybody had to go down and look at the bullet holes."

Chester Clement was a well-known boatbuilder in Southwest Harbor during the '20s and '30s. According to Ralph Stanley, "His boats were awful good-going boats. He built three rum-runners: *Pronto,* in 1929, was maybe fifty feet long, ten feet wide. *Pronto II,* in 1931, was fifty-five or sixty feet long, nearly twelve feet wide. *Maybe,* in 1932, was eighty feet long, and I don't know but what she was fifteen feet wide. She had armor plate in her, a flush deck, and a pilothouse with little windows like Brinks trucks used to have. She had a whole machine shop in her. They could make anything they'd need for the engine. She had big drums for mufflers, and 1,650 horsepower in three airplane engines. They were taking her away to Long Island Sound when the Coast Guard stopped her. 'Course she was registered for fishing.

" 'So you're going fishing?' they asked.

" 'Maybe,' he said, and that's how she got her name.

"But she was caught the first trip," says Ralph. "In 1955 all three of those boats were still registered. They may still be."

Out in Corea, the story was the same, says Arvid Young, who builds fiberglass lobsterboats as a partner in Young Brothers'. "Father ran a lot of it and had one of the fastest boats around. It was a Will Frost thirty-six-footer, a big boat back then, though it was probably no more than eight feet wide. He had a 150-horsepower Kermath straight-line in it. He'd get a half a playing card in the mail with a date on it, and on that day he'd run off and meet them. If the card didn't match, nobody got anything.

"They'd invite my father aboard for supper, or lunch, or whatever it was, while the crew loaded the boat. He'd take it into Hancock or Sullivan or Bar Harbor or wherever they said. Most generally, he'd just go into a beach and leave it. The Coast Guard didn't have a chance; they didn't have the speed. They could do eight knots; Father could do twenty. A lot of people were hauling rum around here. It was hard times. If there was a way you could make a dollar, you did it.

"One boat went ashore on a ledge and broke up, and of course everybody was after the alcohol. Not my father—he was after the engine. He got it home and got it all fixed up, but the Coast Guard confiscated it.

"Then one time in Sorrento harbor, he come into the float, and of course Dad always tied up with a single line amidships. 'How come you do that?' a fellow asked him.

" 'If the authorities show up, I can just put her in gear and part it and be gone,' he said.

" 'Look around you,' the man said. 'You don't have to worry about that.' They were surrounded by armed men, in trucks and on rooftops, carrying those short-barreled guns with the round chamber underneath.

"He went home and told his mother about it. 'Son, it's time to get out of it,' she said.

"My dad said, 'It was the only time I ever really listened to my mother.' "

On Beals Island, Avery Kelley grew up hearing stories about rum running. He particularly likes the one about the revenuers chasing someone in a super fast boat and ending up in a barn. "They tried to make a turn and went in through the boat house," he says. He also enjoys telling the tale of a fisherman who camouflaged the shape of his boat. He knew the revenuers would be looking for a flat-decked vessel, so this fellow made his boat look as if it had a superstructure. "All it was was just liquor crates stacked up," says Avery.

Islesboro's Went Durkee also remembers Prohibition: "They used to get the lobster fishermen to go out after it—course, they'd have to go out beyond the three-mile limit. The Coast Guard used to take chase, and first thing they'd know, they'd run onto a ledge, and the lobster fisherman would be twistin' and turnin' and goin' in some little gully, and he'd leave 'em there, fetched up solid.

"You ever see that Hand Whiskey, in a three-gallon can with what looked like a hand on it? Well, those cans shone some. One time the Coast Guard was chasin' some fishermen, and they swung into Sprague's Beach. It was high tide, so they estimated where low water was, and they throwed it all overboard, figurin' they could gaff it up at low water, and most of them went ashore. Well, 'twas a full moon night, and they'd misjudged low water: them cans was all on the beach, dry and shinin'."

Corliss Holland, now of Belfast, remembers his family's stories, too. "Father was quite a successful rum runner," Corliss says. "You can print that, because everybody's dead now anyway." Corliss's father was captain of a lobster smack for the Consolidated Lobster Company, a Massachusetts firm, and he used the boat a little on the side, going out beyond the three-mile limit and bringing back alcohol to wherever it was going. "One time he knew the Coast Guard boat was going to overhaul him," recalls Corliss, "so he went right over to them and asked them the course into Boston. He figured that if he went alongside, they'd overlook him, and he was right. You know, they had the right course, too!"

BEALS,
Where the Boats Are Born in Them

It's generally accepted that the single most important place in the development of the Maine lobsterboat is Beals Island. And perhaps the two most important people to come to Beals, at least from the point of view of lobsterboats, were Manwaring Beal, who settled the island in 1775, and Will Frost, who appeared in 1914. Descended from Manwaring are literally dozens of boatbuilders, and their craftsmanship and designs, as well as the qualities of many boats built farther west, come down from Will Frost.

Frost arrived on the island (then a part of Jonesport) from Digby, Nova Scotia, and Grand Manan, New Brunswick, before World War I. He saw that Maine would provide a better market for the boats he liked to build. Frost soon grew homesick, however, and took his family back to Nova Scotia for a time. After the war, he returned to Beals and went to building boats that everyone noticed and admired.

It was Will Frost who established the so-called Jonesporter class, whose influence is seen in all modern lobsterboats to one degree or another. "He had the eye for a boat," said his grandson Carroll Lowell. Frost brought extensive boatbuilding experience with him from Canada, and he was happy to teach the local men he hired everything they wanted to learn. Virtually all the well-known boatbuilders and designers of Beals Island are directly descended from Manwaring Beal: Alvin Beal, Mariner Beal, Vinal Beal, Dougie Dodge, Riley Beal, Adrian Beal, Richard Alley, Ernest Libby Jr., Osmond Beal, Calvin Beal

Jr., Freddy Lenfestey, Clifford Alley, Philmore Crowley, Clinton Beal, Willis Beal . . . the list goes on and on. (Only Harold Gower, who came from Canada to work with Frost, wasn't related by blood—and Harold married a descendant of Manwaring's.) Almost every one of these craftsmen worked for Will Frost, or their fathers did, or they worked for someone who had.

By the mid-twentieth century, lobsterboat construction had become a staple of the Beals economy.

At first, the down east lobsterboats had overhung sterns, like the sailing vessels of their time. Later came the torpedo-stern boats, considered by many to be among the most beautiful lobsterboats ever produced. The first one was built in 1905 by Maurice Dow of Roque Bluffs for Eddie Kelley of Jonesport. "The way I heard it," says Willis Beal, "Eddie made a little play-boat with an overhung stern, and he was pulling it from a peapod to see how it'd go. I guess it tipped over and went better, and he thought that was because of the stern. So he asked Maurice Dow if he could build it that way, and Maurice said he guessed he could, but he'd have to have more money to do it."

Boats with the torpedo stern had, in fact, been seen on various lakes in this country and in Europe, so Maine probably cannot be credited with its development. Nonetheless, this feature did lend a glamorous touch to Maine lobsterboats for three decades. The last old-time torpedo-stern boat was built by Will Frost in 1934 for Farrell Lenfestey. Says Willis, "Seems to me that boat—with the motor, ready to go lobstering—cost $1,100 or $1,200. I believe it had a Kermath engine.

"My father owned a boat very similar to that one," Willis recalls. "He had a chance to get a thirty-footer with a cut-off stern, brand new. But he didn't want it, and he got a used torpedo instead. Shows how foolish young folks are.

He thought when people saw one going by with a cut-off stern, they'd say, 'What a lookin' sight that is; that'll never catch on.' "

Many believe that Frost was the first to use the square stern in a lobster-boat. "There were a couple or three boatbuilders in the beginning," says Avery Kelley, himself a descendant of Manwaring on his mother's side, "but Will Frost was an experimenter. He hired quite a few people, and he was willing to help you out. He didn't want to be smarter than anyone else.

"I don't know as they classify him as one of the better boatbuilders," Avery admits, noting that perhaps Frost took some shortcuts that the purists wouldn't approve of. But Avery is quick to acknowledge Frost's skill at lofting—drawing out boat plans full size on a wooden floor. "His son, Bert, was a very respected boatbuilder," notes Avery. "He learned geometry and algebra, and that was quite a help in drafting, where his father didn't have a clue." Grandson Carroll Lowell concurred: "Gramps would make a model, then they'd take calipers and hang them off the model and loft it out. Whatever [problems] they didn't pick up on the loft floor, they'd pick up in fairing the framing."

Today, the trucks and the boats are bigger, but these rigs are still a common sight on the island's roads.

In other words, Frost's design work was a hands-on process: First, he sawed, planed, and sanded a small-scale wooden model until the shape of the boat was right. Then, he measured it, converted the measurements to full scale and laid them out on the floor. Finally, he used long battens—narrow strips of clear, straight wood—and an educated eye to make sure that the lofted lines and, later, the erected frames defined fair (smooth) curves.

Will Frost's boats were known to be fast. "He built a few rum runners," Avery says. "They were fifty-six feet long, with tremendous horsepower—brutal things. Then he designed one for the government to catch them. You'd think the guy would have died wealthy, but he'd be broke and then he'd get on and then he'd be broke again." Frost's business on Beals finally failed once too often, and he moved around after that—from Rhode Island to Massachusetts to southern Maine—building boats until 1953. But his influence is seen all along the Maine coast, in the sheerlines that are accepted as the traditional look of a lobsterboat, and in the construction details and underwater shapes, as well.

Thanks, in large part, to Frost, the business of building lobsterboats blossomed on Beals Island. Many fishermen started boats in the winter, often out in the weather. They had no trouble selling them off-island, because there was such a demand for the new-style boat. In the '50s and '60s, some Beals men were building three or four lobsterboats a year. "None of these fellows had any schooling other than what they picked up from somebody else," says Avery. "Ernest Libby, one of the finest names there is, never went to high school. A lot of them never did. If you was a lobster fisherman, you knew what to do to make a lobster boat better. It's just like it was born in them. Just like a Labrador retriever knows to go to the water and start swimmin', these fellows knew how to grab a piece of cedar and go to planin'."

Each of the Beals Island builders had his own way, his own style of detailing, but anyone who knows about these things can tell a traditional Beals boat—there's a look about them. They are skeg-built and low sided, with a graceful sheerline, beautiful angles, and great balance. Most Beals Islanders can distinguish the work of one island builder from that of another.

"Harold Gower was supposedly the best, the Cadillac," says Avery. "Of course, he was a connection of Frost's: his mother and Mrs. Frost were sisters. He wanted things a little bit better. His boats was a little bit more expensive, but they was just like a yacht, every seam recessed. You could take one of them to New Jersey and sell it as a yacht just as good as them coming out of Southwest Harbor or Northeast. He liked playin' with mahogany—kind of dressed up the boat. He took a lot of pride. If the workmen didn't do it right, sometimes after hours he'd do it again." Gower was also responsible for some clever innovations: improvements in the stuffing box (where the propeller shaft passes through the hull) and many other modifications to make the water flow more smoothly under the hull or make the boat more attractive. Avery remembers Harold Gower with affection. "Never once did he give us kids a hard time," he says.

Like most of the boatbuilders on Beals, Harold Gower enjoyed what he was doing. "I like boatbuilding," he once said, "and I'll build till I can't."

"When those fellers got old, they got real stubborn," Avery says. He explains that Harold had raised Dougie Dodge (himself a fourth great-grandson of Manwaring Beal), and Dougie worked with him in the shop for years. "In the last boat that Gower built, Dougie wanted him to widen out the stern, but Harold just couldn't do it," recalls Avery. "He'd been building boats all his life, and they'd never had such a wide stern." After Harold left the shop for the day, Dougie set up the stern with the extra width he wanted. When Harold came back, he planked it; he just couldn't make himself frame up the wider shape.

"The only bad thing was these people built such a good boat in wood," says Avery, "that when fiberglass came out, they didn't want to build with it. You don't know how stubborn those guys were."

But the Beals design was finally put into 'glass. "If I had gone into fiber-

The traditional Beals model features low sides with a pronounced upward curve in the rail.

glass," says Avery, "I would have taken the prettiest, most popular wood boat, and I'd have made a mold from it. That's just what Youngs did, over in Corea. They got a Beals Island boat that belonged to a local fellow and offered to fix it all up for him if they could use it as the plug for a mold. Well, they couldn't build them fast enough."

And so it was that some of the Beals Island boats became forms, or "plugs," over which were built laminated-fiberglass "female" molds. The 'glass hulls themselves were then built, or "laid up," inside this "tooling" using layers of resin-saturated fiberglass fabric and, sometimes, a reinforcing core of balsa or foam.

After introducing their first model, the Young brothers—Arvid, Arvin, and Colby—hired Ernest Libby Jr. to design the rest of their boats. "Nernie, he had nothin'," says Avery, "but he was buildin' boats for this person and that, and then he got designin', and now he's doin' real well." Thus the Beals Island lobster-boat tradition continued, in a changed form.

Just a few years ago, Willis Beal, fourth great-grandson of Manwaring, built two torpedo-stern boats whose lines were only somewhat modified from those of Will Frost's original model. "One's got a house, and a fellow works her," says Avery Kelley. "The other one belongs to a fellow with a lot of money, comes in the summer. She's got everything in her—the crane and everything—but she'll never haul a trap. They use her to go back and forth to the island. He loves the thing. Sometimes when they're having a party, they'll trailer her to Rhode Island just so he can take people around down there. They did it two or three times last summer. Think nothing of it."

Not many wooden boats are built on Beals any more. Avery explains that most of the activity involves fabricating plugs and molds used for fiberglass boats and finishing off 'glass hulls. "Gower was right," asserts Avery. "He said, 'The fiberglass boats may last, but the guys buildin' them won't.' And he's right. Workin' that stuff's bad for you."

Most Maine fishermen aren't using the traditional Jonesport/Beals designs these days. But respect and affection for the older style boats lives on, as it does in Bob and Linda Achorn. The Achorns live on Islesboro and now fish together from a Nova Scotia–built boat. "I picked crabs for fifteen years," says Linda, "then I semi-retired and went lobsterin'. I'd had enough of those dead bodies." The couple now fishes 150 traps. The smallest dog I've ever seen in my life goes with them.

The Achorns used to own an old Harold Gower boat. They bought her from the late Les Smith Sr., who had named her the *Mr. Knapp* for his next-door neighbor in Connecticut. "It was a nice boat," Bob says. "It sliced right through the water. I hated to part with that boat, but it was just gettin' to be a lot of work."

"And tax-wise, we had to sell it," Linda says. "It was paid for."

"I wouldn't mind having a brand-new one just like it," Bob says. "This one I got now is a good boat, a real seaworthy boat, but it goes *over* everything. It's so fat—and fat well forward—you have to slow down when the water's rough. With the *Mr. Knapp* you could cruise right along; it'd just cut right through. I've come across the bay when it was some ugly. One time I come across after a load of champagne—"

"The champagne wasn't for us!" Linda interrupts. "One of the summer people was havin' a party, and the truck had missed the ferry, or maybe it wasn't runnin'. Heaven forbid they should have a party without booze!"

"Nobody could even see me from the shore," Bob says, "between the waves." Linda agrees.

"Goin' through the water, you could see her work," Bob says, referring to the flexing that afflicts many older wooden boats when they're driven hard. "Of course those Jonesport boats did work some, anyway, but Les had used her for scallopin', and that strained her. She had some of that fiberglass sheathing on her, and when I took it off, I could push the planks right off her with my feet. That fiberglass was all that was holdin' her together. I think I put a couple of ribs in her after that."

The Achorns sold the *Mr. Knapp* to Avery Stone, who changed her name to *Gower's Grace*. "She wanted that boat for years," the Achorns told me.

Avery admits it. "She's so beautiful," she says. "I've had my eye on her for twenty years, but she kept being snapped up by one fisherman after another." Avery is having *Gower's Grace* restored, and one of these days, the Harold Gower boat will be back on the bay, as good as new.

"The lobsterboat is as synonymous with coastal living as woodpiles in the fall or black flies come spring."

—Jim Rockefeller, Camden

The Lobsterboat from a Yacht Yard

In the late 1950s, Jim Rockefeller moved to Camden and, as he feels was certain to happen, went in search of the perfect lobsterboat. He found his boat on Matinicus, from which island she had been making a living for a decade. Jim renamed her the *Mandalay*. She was built in 1948 by, of all people, Malcolm Brewer of Camden Shipbuilding, well known as a builder of fine yachts like the elegant little Murray Peterson schooners that proved so popular along the coast. Malcolm may not have turned his hand to a lobsterboat before, but he had no difficulty taking the model given him and building a working boat. They say that at $6,200 she was the most expensive lobsterboat built to date in the state of Maine, but she was constructed solidly and is still alive today.

The boat was built for Harold Bunker, a Matinicus fisherman from the time he was a young man until he retired when he was sixty-five. He called her the *Albert and Vance* after his two sons. When asked why he hired Brewer, Harold says in his unassuming way, "He was s'posed to build pretty good boats. Somebody recommended him to me; I don't remember who. No, I don't believe he had built a lobsterboat before. But he built another one afterwards. She was s'posed to be just the same, but she was altogether a different boat."

The *Albert and Vance* was constructed of fir planking on oak frames, the fir being left over from the minesweepers that had been built in Camden during World War II. "That fir was very heavy," Harold says. "When you were out, and it was rough, and you'd go into those chops, she'd just bury her bow."

"She was a submarine when it was rough," agrees Rena, Harold's wife.

"The other one Malcolm built was planked with cedar and was a lot better boat," says Harold.

He tells a story about the *Albert and Vance*. "I was out hauling traps back of Wooden Ball," says Harold, "and my son Albert was headed back from Malcolm Ledge, bound for Matinicus Rock. I see him coming, and of course I s'posed he was going to slip alongside for a gam. But he kept coming, and first thing I knew, he come right through the stern of my boat."

The **Albert and Vance** *was planked with dense fir originally intended for minesweeper construction.*

Albert says, "I was sitting on the washboard having my lunch, and I never even saw my dad. Jeez, the next thing, I looked up and saw the fire in his eyes. I ran off and left him."

Harold headed home, too, and to prevent the *Albert and Vance* from sinking, he kept her going full tilt. "And then," says Albert, "halfway in, I ran out of gas, and *he* had to tow *me* in."

Albert paid to have the boat fixed up, and Harold says he wasn't angry with his son. Still, he admits, "She was brand new—it kinda hurt your feelings, you know."

Jim Rockefeller, the boat's third owner, describes asking the second, Clyde Young, if there wasn't a compass aboard the boat. "He pointed to a white box nailed to the main bulkhead, remarking that it was little used," says Jim. "Sure enough, there it lay encased, all of eight inches in diameter, made even more imposing by the three dynamite caps lying under the bowl.

"Placing them swiftly but gingerly in his pocket Clyde casually remarked, 'Been a little trouble down here, lately.' "

The *Albert and Vance* ran into some father-and-son difficulty a second time, after she was renamed the *Mandalay*. The Rockefellers were on Vinalhaven one night when Jim's son had an overwhelming urge for pizza and headed for Carver's Harbor in the boat. Along the way, he ran the *Mandalay* aground and tore the stem out of her. Murray Hopkins of Vinalhaven put her back together; Jim speaks of telling Hopkins how sad he was that after all these years of hard work, the boat had gone aground and been badly damaged. "Save the stem," Jim says he told Hopkins, "because I'm going to hang it over my son's bed."

"If it was my son," Hopkins retorted, "I'd take it and jam it up his ass."

The *Mandalay* now belongs to Frank O'Hara of Rockland and has had some further work done on her. Clearly, the boat takes after Harold Bunker, her first owner, in longevity. He's in his nineties; Rena expects him to live to be a hundred. There's no telling how long the *Mandalay* will be around, but like her first owner, she's still going.

Built in 1948 for fisherman Harold Bunker, the Brewer-built boat is still going strong today.

RALPH STANLEY
Continuing a Southwest Harbor Tradition

I go up to the front door, under the carved sign that announces *Ralph Stanley's Boat Shop*, and look in through the glass. Stuff is piled right up against the door. This obviously isn't the way in. Around on the side I find another door, but there's no one in the office anyway.

Boards and planks and scraps of wood are stacked alongside the alleyway that leads to the shop itself. Here, a young man working on a graceful sailboat hull tells me that Ralph is down on the dock. Climbing around spars and oars and a skiff, I track him down. He's a compact, tidy-looking man, with short-cropped gray hair. He's dressed in khaki and wears a baseball cap that says *Ralph W. Stanley, Inc.* He leads me back up to the office. There, we sit around a big desk piled high with papers and magazines and who-knows-what, surrounded by boxes of fastenings, shelves of paint, and cabinets. But every time Ralph wants to find anything—the book about him or the *Newsweek* article or a copy of his advertising blurb or the Friendship Sloop Days program from last year—he unhesitatingly puts his hand right on it.

When Ralph was a youngster, his father had a double-ender, typical of the times, with just a spray hood on the bow. "He broke down one night in 1935. It was overcast and had looked like snow all day. On his way back, in the gut between two of the Cranberry Islands, the generator played out, and the boat stopped. She was adrift. The wind came in northwest, and in the course of the evening, blew a gale.

"He lit a flare with gasoline and some rags in a bucket, and the Coast

Guard station at Islesford saw him and tried to go out to get him. But their lifeboat was up; all they had was a buoy tender of twenty-five feet. It wasn't very seaworthy, and it iced up, and they had to go in." Ralph explains that all the lighthouses were still manned in those days. "Duck Island saw his flares, and later Baker Island, and finally Mount Desert Rock could see them. His anchor eventually fetched up on Northern Peak shoal, this side of Mount Desert Rock.

"It was awful cold. The temperature was five degrees below zero here. Might not have been quite that cold out there. He frostbit his fingers—had no gloves—and what clothes he did have was wet. He knew he shouldn't go to sleep. That open boat, she'd roll right down to the water, and he had to brace himself just to stay inside.

"Everyone thought he was gone."

The next morning Ralph's father was found and brought in by a fisherman from Bass Harbor. "The Islesford station had a shakeup after that. Everybody was transferred, and they brought in a whole new crew. They shouldn't have had the lifeboat out of the water without a backup."

Not all of Ralph Stanley's early memories were so harrowing, but—not surprisingly—many of them involve boats and boatbuilding. "The old-time builders I knew as a boy, they built on their own model and wouldn't build on anyone else's. Theirs was always the best. Each man took great pride in his own model; they were always experimenting with them, playing, trying to get them better. Even as kids they built little sailboats and played with them in puddles— I did that, too. Now you don't see it.

"Around here, there were eight or ten people building boats then. They always built down, on a keel. In Jonesport the boats were all built on a skeg. Nova Scotia boats were built down, too. Maybe the people here were influenced by pleasure boats that came up from the west. One thing about a built-down boat, you can pump her out from the cockpit. A skeg boat you have to pump out from the cabin. It's kind of unhandy, if you're using a bucket."

In 1951, Ralph Stanley built his first boat, for himself. He used her to commute to a job on the Cranberry Islands and did a little handlining on her. It took him two winters to build her. "I didn't have any money, and I didn't know what I was doing. When I finally got it finished, I thought, 'Gorry, I'm glad that's done,' and I thought I'd never have enough courage to start another. But when a fellow wanted me to build one, I couldn't wait to get started. I've been building them ever since."

The boat Ralph owns today, the *Seven Girls,* is on the ways outside his shop. Ralph built her for his father in 1960; she had five other owners after Chester Stanley died, and now she's come back home. She was the first of the boats he built from a model for a thirty-two footer. "Every boat I built on that model was thirty-three feet long," he says with a grin. "And I built five or six of them.

"The fellow who bought my first thirty-five-foot boat used her for lobstering and trawling and also handlining pollock. One trip he brought in 15,000 pounds of pollock, all back of the bulkhead. The stern wasn't even down in the water as far as the name. If you loaded some boats with 13,000 pounds, you'd slap a fish in, and another would slide right off over the stern. They'd be all the way down in the water.

"That first thirty-five is down to Christmas Cove now, in South Bristol, and she's still going."

Ralph Stanley's boats have their own distinctive look, featuring well balanced proportions throughout.

Ralph notes with regret that few working lobsterboats are long lived. "Most fishermen aren't ones to take care of their boats; they just use them. Last month, I started working on a lobsterboat that Raymond Bunker built thirty-two years ago. It needed some caulking down the garboard, and I took care of that. Then he said there was some trouble with the rudder. Well, the rudder was broken, the post was just worn out, the rudder step was worn out—everything was all adrift. He got a new rudder post, and I made a new rudder for him.

"The stuffing box was all loose—he had beat that thing up. The boat had an inch-and-a-half shaft, but an inch-and-three-quarters would've fit in there. The hanging bolts on the stern post were so corroded they just broke off, and I had to drill them all out. There I was on my back under that boat, drilling; it took eight or nine hours to bore those out. It just shows you: in thirty-two years, that guy'd never looked at that stern post. Ten years ago, you could have taken those bolts right out.

"Finally, yesterday, I got him all fixed up. But his boat still needs a lot of work. She could be saved, if you did it now, but he's in his seventies. I doubt he'll be needing her much longer; he'll just use her. Today that boat would cost him $150,000, maybe more. Probably cost him six or eight thousand, thirty-two years ago."

Is there a way to tell a Ralph Stanley boat from another builder's? He laughs. "Well, I can tell! But every boat's a little different. I always build a boat a little different. I did have one guy who wanted one just the same, and it was pretty close. But it's subtle, the differences.

"There's more lobsterboats in this harbor built by me than any other single builder. There's the forty-four-footer *Barbara and Carol*, the thirty-three-footer *Wandabob*, the thirty-seven-footer *Frances Inez*—my nephew owns her—the thirty-one-foot *Betty* … something. There's a lot of them.

"I always liked to build lobsterboats. It's a fairly simple boat to build, there's not a lot of detail, and you get a lot of satisfaction out of seeing a boat working, contributing to the economy, doing some people some good."

WENT DURKEE
on Lobstering, Mid-Century

From the dock, Phil and I walk up-island along Islesboro's main road, and everyone who passes us raises a couple of fingers from the steering wheel. We don't know a one of them. The island is fourteen miles long and a mile wide at its widest point. Except in summer, everyone knows everyone. No doubt they all took note of our boat, a stranger tied up to the float where the familiar *Owl* is moored, waiting for Wentworth Durkee to take the wheel.

Went is mowing the lawn when we get to his house. I've only seen him a few times in the thirty years since we summered down the road from him. He doesn't look much different, though he's over eighty. He turns off the mower, commenting that things are coming together. "Didn't know if the sweet peas would ever come up, but they poked through, finally. Come over in the boat, did you?"

We did.

"Well, come on in," he says, and leads us into the kitchen, where the big wood cookstove is well fired up. His wife, Edna, is at the table and motions for us to sit down. Everyone asks how everyone else has come through the winter, and—determining that we all are reasonably healthy now—I get on to why we came.

"I'd like to hear about lobstering," I tell Went.

He obliges.

"When we married, moved up here—"

"That was the first day of May 1938," Edna puts in.

41

"I had a rowboat and ten traps. That was enough to make the payments on the house. Caught my own bait—there was fish around then. In a half hour you could catch enough flounder and sculpin to bait ten traps. Sold lobsters to Miss Grace [Went's father was her caretaker] at 50 cents a pound."

Edna breaks in again. The fellow they bought their house from had a shack down on the Lime Kiln point. "He'd worry about Went out in the fog; he'd sit down there and pound on somethin', makin' a noise." She shakes her head. "He was afraid Went wouldn't find his way home in the fog." The idea was clearly foolish to them both.

"I always dreamt of having a string of lobster traps all the way round the island," Went goes on, "so I could see my first and last trap when I went out in the morning. When Miss Grace died, I bought that first boat, the *Isabel.* I paid three hundred dollars for her, with the understanding that the engine would run. It ran all right, ran when I sold her, too. But God damn, didn't that thing leak! There was no automatic bilge pumps in those days. I pumped her every hour, by hand, into a bucket. The pump had a wood shaft and a leather gasket.

"Then I got the *Edna.* She was a handy little boat, built in Stonington at Billings, but she was the Riley Beal design—he was workin' there then. She was wet—she was something like a submarine—but by God, she was able. I hammered her up from Owls Head one time—been scallopin'. It took four hours. Man ain't got any brains, has he? In fifteen minutes I could've been in the lee behind Owls Head. Nobody but a damn fool like me would have gone scallopin' in the middle of the ocean in such a little boat anyway. I used to drag off the government racecourse down there, where they got them buoys set out [to measure boat speed]. I brought up a candlestick and cups and everythin'. I guess they didn't want to wash dishes, so they'd just pitch 'em."

"That candlestick was perfect, not a thing wrong with it, a real nice candlestick," Edna says.

"I scalloped six winters," Went continues. "It was a long run, but there was nothing up in the bay. You had to go down to Owls Head and out to Two Bush. The water out there's 501 feet deep in one place. There was more than twenty boats scallopin' then—lobsterboats, herring seiners—everybody wanted to go scallopin'. I guess I was the smallest boat out there.

"I used to get just forty cents a pound for them damn things—you had to sink the boat with them to pay for the gas. They get six or seven dollars, now. Course, they got some better equipment than we had.

"Nobody ever tells you nothin'. You got to learn for yourself. The first time I towed a drag, I dismasted. Then I had a hell of a long spell of landing my drag on the bottom upside down. I did it fourteen times one day, and then I told my sternman, 'This time, when it comes aboard, for God's sake, land it on its feet!' Then he took the wheel, and I stood right there and cut the back out of that drag. I knit a new one, here in this kitchen, and that drag never went upside down again. An old feller here said to me, 'Well, I could 'a' told you—that thing looked like a fat woman with a set of tight corsets on.' Well, it didn't look like that any more. It looked like her corsets had loosened up some. But you have to learn for yourself."

"And then there was the time you lost the lobster car," reminds Edna, referring to the floating, tethered wooden crate into which many lobstermen put their catch at the end of each day, holding them until the price or the weather is right for a trip to the buyer.

VIRGINIA L. THORNDIKE

Went Durkee

"Day before Christmas, the car let go, and eight hundred pounds of lobsters escaped," says Went. "Well, I went out and set a hundred traps right there in the cove. I'd 'a' done better with half that many—there was so much bait, they all fed fine without gettin' in the traps. I was catchin' them lobsters all spring—caught the last of them over by Gadd's on Memorial Day weekend. They don't crawl far, lobsters. They was all pegged, you know—there I was catchin' pegged lobsters!" (Lobstermen used to disarm the lobsters' big claws with a peg. Now they use a rubber band.)

Phil is looking at the wood stove he's sitting next to. "We just bought that stove," Went says. "It's a rebuilt one. Paid more for it than for the whole house—

$800. Only paid $650 for the house and eight acres. House is one of the old-est ones on the island—not the oldest, but one of the first frame houses."

We've gotten away from boats and fishing, and we turn the conversation back that way. "That green boat, the *Edna,* she was a handy little thing. Once you got her set up, you could stand on one foot and work her all day long. You could row up to her and throw your bait into her; you didn't have to heave it way up in the air like you do with them new boats now. Them high sides are only good for falling out of.

"People don't realize now what went into fishin' then. After I got 300 traps, I had to spend a hundred days in the winter repairing them. Had to build about fifty new ones. One year, I had my 300 traps, and there were two bows and some lath left over. So, I went out in my yard and cut a little cedar, bent it round into the third bow, and made one more trap. Then I had 301. Well, I set that trap out off what's now the town beach, and I never saw it again till five years later. I was down that way, and there it was on a fellow's doorstep, buoy and warp and all. He must 'a' pulled it within a couple of hours after I set it.

"Nowadays they all fish wire traps and don't have to do nothin' but just tie a rope on 'em. But now you gotta have a number plate on 'em; you got to reg-ister 'em. Randy, my grandson, is going to fish 1,000 traps this summer. He fig-ures he's going to pay for his boat, I guess. I used to fish 247 traps, completely around the island, and sometimes got in with just three small lobsters. Now, if they don't get a dozen in every trap, they're disappointed. Well, last summer, Randy paid his sternman a goodly sum one week, and the damn fool didn't know enough to keep his mouth shut. Now every painter and every carpenter's going lobster fishing.

"People are funny," he says. "When I was lobsterin', Edna was home all the time, and she'd sell lobsters to anybody that wanted them—all they had to do was call. But people used to holler to me from the shore, wantin' to buy lob-sters, expectin' me to come right in onto the shore. When I heard 'em hollerin' I'd turn up the radio so I couldn't hear 'em any more. And one time, 'bout ten o'clock at night, I was settin' down to supper when the phone rang. 'How many lobsters you think I could eat?' the fellow wants to know. 'I don't know,' I says, 'but hungry's I am, I could eat a dozen,' and I hung up the phone.

"Lobsterin' was hard work, but I liked it," says Went. "One thing about working on the water, ain't no two days the same." He adds, "Anyone hasn't seen the sun rise out of the water hasn't lived. It's the most beautiful sight you ever saw."

"Growing up during the Depression was one of the most important points of my education. There was a communal spirit that has disappeared since. Nobody had any money, and everyone pitched in. If a neighbor was down and out, people would bring in his hay and cut his wood and make sure he was all right. I don't want those times to come back, but they didn't hurt me. Taught me to appreciate everything I had."

—Boatbuilder Arno Day, Sedgwick

ARNO DAY
Staying with Wood and Having Fun

Arno Day greets us at the door of his small frame house and directs us to chairs around a table that takes up most of the space in the room. There's a drafting table behind me, and there are rolls of boat plans and piles of related books and magazines on all horizontal surfaces. Arno moves slowly and with no excess motion. He speaks the same way.

"A lot of boatbuilders switched to fiberglass because that's how to make a living at it. You can hire inexperienced people and put them right to work. But I was born too long ago to get involved in fiberglass, so I stayed in wood and had fun." He started building lobsterboats with his father and brother in the fall of 1945, and although he hasn't built a lobsterboat in a while, he's always apt to be working on a small boat of some sort. "I can draw just about so long, and then I have to go out and whittle on something," he says.

Recently Arno has become interested in plywood, and his present project is a plywood peapod for his grandchildren. Later on, he takes us out to his shop, where a succession of lobsterboat half-models lies on a jig for a flat-bottomed skiff; all are works in progress. It's clear that Arno Day has had fun designing and building boats over the years, and that he continues to.

"There's lots of stuff cropping up in boatbuilding," he says. "Cold molding, for instance." In this process, thin strips of wood are saturated with resin and laid up in several diagonally oriented layers over a male plug. Done properly, it results in a very strong, lightweight, low-maintenance boat.

"That uses epoxy, of course, and my experience with epoxy in the '50s left me allergic to it. We didn't use all the precautions they do today. I was partners with Joel White, and a fellow came in and wanted us to build a lobsterboat and cover it with fiberglass. Because we were one of the first in this area to do anything like that, the company that made the resin thought it would be a good idea to have a seminar about it. They invited all the builders around, and the company man rolled up his sleeves and proceeded to get covered in epoxy. Then he said, 'That's all there is to it.'

"So we went at it, too, and three days later we were the sorriest-looking crew imaginable. One fellow woke up in the morning and couldn't open his eyes—the lids were stuck shut. 'Course the catalyst at that time was really rank, poisonous stuff. Now they use something different, but once it builds up in your body, you just can't stand being around it. If they get to sanding epoxy, I get to itching all over and have to get out of there."

So, in moving beyond traditional plank-on-frame construction, Arno Day has skipped the cold-molding method of building boats with wood and has gone directly—if belatedly—to plywood. He has developed a series of hard-chine plywood designs, ranging from an eighteen-foot skiff to a pair of larger, nearly traditional-looking lobsterboats—one with a displacement hull, the other with a planing hull.

"There's only one guy building wooden lobsterboats any more, really, and that's Peter Kass. He's a great guy. His boats are all big, and they go offshore. I helped Peter with a design a few years ago. He asked me if I could draw the lines from a model he'd made, and I asked him what it would have for power. 'A six-hundred-horsepower diesel,' he told me. It was going to cost $38,000!" exclaims Arno.

"I've argued with a lot of lobster fishermen for hours. What they've done is gone to a planing boat when 90 percent of the time they're idling or jogging around along the shore. But, they're happy with it, so I guess I should be. I've found lobster fishermen to be really fine people to work with and for, but they all have certain ideas they want to incorporate in their boats. They all want a certain measurement from the deck to the coaming, so it'll hit just above the knee. That's usually twenty-one inches, 'cept if someone six-foot-four comes along; he'd want twenty-four inches.

"If you listen very carefully to what they say and build it into their boat, they go away very happy with a smile on their face. My willingness to go along kept me very busy. I built whatever they wanted, skeg-built or built-down."

Just once, a fisherman told Arno to build him a boat any way Arno wanted to. "I always felt I could modify the lobsterboat some and make it easier to build and therefore less expensive. I had this in mind for some time, but

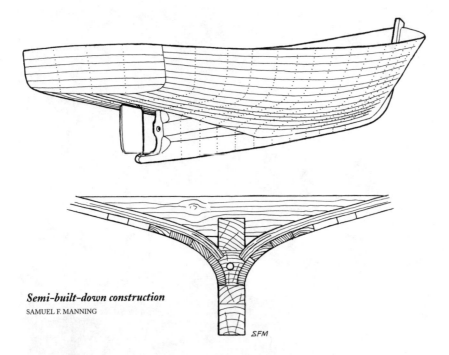

Semi-built-down construction
SAMUEL F. MANNING

I didn't really want to approach a lobsterman who had ideas of his own." Here was his chance. Arno explained to the man in detail what he had in mind.

"That fellow thought a little, and then he says, 'I'm a fisherman, and you're a boatbuilder. You build the boat, and I'll fish it.'"

The new model went over well, and almost all of the lobsterboats Arno built after that were semi-built-down, or semi-skeg. Arno tells of a fisherman from South Thomaston who stopped by with a friend to see how his boat was coming along. "His friend looked the boat over, and asked, 'You call that a skeg boat, or a built-down?'

"'Charlie,' said the fisherman, 'You look real careful, you'll see she's semi-skeg on one side, and semi-built-down on the other.'

"But by then," Arno continues, "the cat was pretty well out of the bag, and it was accepted." Some fishermen, he explains, like one term better than the other. "In ten minutes, you can tell if a fellow's a skeg man or a built-down type," he says, chuckling. "If you can do that without laughing."

Arno Day is one of several Maine designer/builders who successfully developed the basic lobsterboat design for recreational use. But it wasn't a simple task. "At first, it was difficult to make a good pleasure boat on a lobsterboat model. You go to a boat show, and people have two questions they ask: 'How many does it sleep?' and 'How fast does it go?' A Chris-Craft can sleep six on twenty-six feet, but it takes a while to get folks to understand you can't do that on a lobsterboat hull. For instance, you've got that engine box right where you need the room for accommodations. But I got the bright idea of

Arno Day at his drawing board

moving the engine farther back and running it through a V-drive. I built several that way.

"And the fiberglass boys are working out how to make a nice pleasure boat on a lobsterboat hull. They've made it higher, to give it more headroom. And people don't give much thought to the amount of gas the boat uses as long as they're having fun.

"Nobody's building a real displacement boat any more, but there's a demand for it," Arno says. "People who've been sailing all their lives are happy at sailing speeds. One guy wanted a twenty-eight-foot boat that could get to hull speed with a six-horsepower Volvo diesel motor. He made a date to come talk about it, but I never saw him. Maybe he lost his courage.

"I like to tell people who want to go fast that they should get in their car and go just's fast as they can, and then go on the water and do what the water is designed to do, and listen to the water swish and the birds howl. But they don't hear.

" 'Course I grew up with one-cylinder engines—my grandfather was an agent for the three-horsepower Hartford single-cylinder engine. Had no reduction gear or reverse gears to bother with. It would go either way." Arno explains what was involved in starting the motor. "You'd rock it back and forth and get it just right, and it'd go bang," he says. "The old-timers used it as a reverse gear. When they were coming into the dock, they'd kill the motor and then watch the flywheel. When it got to the right place, they'd set her going again, and they'd have a reverse gear."

He chuckles. "At least, 90 percent of the time, they would. There's an old joke says that's why all the small wharves that used to be around the shore have disappeared.

"What's so interesting about boats is there's so many different shapes, you can get all tangled up," Arno says. "I was subjected to boats since I was that high," holding his hand a foot off the floor. "I'm the fourth generation building boats, and my son is teaching boatbuilding down in New Brunswick now. I couldn't talk him out of it. Soon's I was big enough to toddle, I spent a lot of time in my grandfather's shop. Whenever I got to driving nails where I shouldn't, he'd give me a piece of pine and tell me to whittle a boat. Every one of them, he'd show me where it was wrong. I never could get it just right. One time I said to him, 'I can't make this side the same as the other.'

"He said, 'All you can do is keep trying. If you get to the point where you think you've done something that's perfect, hang up your tools.' "

More and more people around the coast of Maine are coming to Arno to learn how to build more nearly perfect boats. He lectures at the museums and apprentice-shops, and he teaches courses at the WoodenBoat School in nearby Brooklin. And all the present and future boatbuilders who've benefited from his advice are very glad that Arno Day hasn't hung up his tools.

"I've seen times on a real foggy day, you couldn't run ashore if you wanted to, because all the ledges are used up. There's a sailboat on every one of them."

—Gweeka Williams, Vinalhaven

The Lobsterboat As Tug

The *Double B* chugs out of Northeast Harbor in the fog, pushing a barge with a full gravel truck aboard. She's skippered by David Bunker of Beal and Bunker, Inc., a company that has carried mail, commuters, and freight to the Cranberry Isles for more than forty years.

"Clarence Beal is long gone, now," David says, "but we kept the name. Father and I are the company now, and he's semi-retired—he doesn't work so much anymore. He goes to Florida in the winter and lets me worry about things. I've been doing this ever since I finished high school and got my license in '69. I'd been deckhanding on the boats since I was eleven or twelve years old, and I was running the smaller boats with freight when I was still in high school. You don't need a license unless you're carrying passengers for hire.

"Clarence was a fisherman who had a wooden boat he used for lobstering winters, and father had a boat. So, summers, they put them together, chartering and that. Father had a little landing craft—it would take a car or a truck. They had as many as five boats, one time. They ran a wooden barge, and then in '74 we had this steel one built." Now Beal and Bunker has three boats, the forty-four-foot wooden *Sea Queen*, the thirty-eight-foot wooden *Double B,* and the thirty-four-foot fiberglass *Captain B.*

The company runs the mail and a regularly scheduled passenger and freight service out to Great Cranberry, Islesford, and Sutton Island, as well as offering barge service and private chartering. On this summer day, we're along for the ride while David takes a dump truck full of gravel out to Great Cranberry.

The *Double B* was purchased in '84. "Chummy Rich in Bass Harbor was building her on spec," David explains. She was no different from any lobsterboat in hull form, but when the Bunkers agreed to buy her, the yard immedi-

51

ately started working with the Coast Guard so that she would be finished according to their requirements for carrying passengers. Presently, the *Double B* is David's boat of choice to push the barge, because she has the largest engine, but she is also licensed to carry forty-nine people. For that kind of service, the Coast Guard required watertight bulkheads, certain types of wiring, and specific reinforcement in the deck, or platform, so that the boat could safely carry the weight of that many passengers.

David Bunker at the helm

"They'd come by every so often and check to see that everything was the way they wanted it, so we wouldn't get it all built and then find out something's wrong. Then, when the boat was finished, there was a stability test: You take the weight of the number of passengers you want to carry—we used 100-pound bags of salt—and you distribute it around the boat. Then you take half of it, put it down the middle, and put the other half on one side. If the scuppers aft are still ten inches above the water, then you're all right. And, of course, the Coast Guard inspects the boat every year and checks the hull in dry dock regularly, too."

The *Double B* has a 220-horsepower John Deere diesel, which David describes as economical and trustworthy, adding that service is available nearby. The engine wouldn't quite fit entirely under the deck—"there would have been just enough to trip over," David says—so the yard built the box up so it could be used as seating. The fuel tank is beneath the deck. David normally refuels every other day in Northeast, directly from a truck. "Sometimes if I'm low," explains David, "the driver'll back right onto the barge, run the hose out and fill me right up.

"Right now, I prefer this boat for barging—she has a little more power. But next year, I hope to put the same engine in the *Captain B.* I switch boats and use her for pushing the barge now, too, if we have a charter for more than the forty people she's licensed for." David says he would rather use the 'glass boat for barging because he thinks its composite hull can handle the stresses better than a wooden one. "Wood's way ahead," he says, "except for that one purpose. As far as going out in rough sea conditions, a wooden boat is far more comfortable and a lot quieter, too. A 'glass boat with a diesel engine under it is like a drum. But fiberglass has its good points too."

We're making four or five knots pushing the barge, David estimates. For today's project, two trucks are taking turns: David takes one truck out, the driver drives off the barge, dumps his load, and returns for the ride back. All the while, the second truck is going to Lamoine for more gravel. "Which one gets back into Northeast first depends on the road traffic; with normal traffic, we do it in just about the same time."

The diesel-powered **Double B** *pushes an inter-island barge carrying a loaded gravel truck.*

This barge is a deck barge, David explains, so any passengers have to ride on the boat; the truck driver and David's deckhand, his cousin Arthur, are in the cabin with us. The driver jokes with David as we approach the shore at Great Cranberry, then he climbs along the side deck to the bow of the *Double B,* down two steps onto the barge, then up into his truck. The big lobsterboat pushes her barge in, its long ramps extending forward so that the truck can drive off onto the island's launch ramp.

There's a notch where the bow of the *Double B* sets into the barge, and cable that ties the two vessels together leads back amidships. David reaches out his door and loosens the line to the cable. As the truck drives off, the barge rises several feet at its outboard end, then settles level again. Now, relieved of its 60,000-pound load, it sits noticeably higher than before.

Nearby, the *Sea Queen* is at the dock at Great Cranberry, unloading passengers, bicycles, boxes, baby-strollers, and you-name-it. "She was built by my Uncle Raymond in 1972," David says. "She's forty-four feet long and twelve feet wide. He built several others—pleasure boats—on the same hull. The cabin structures and all the comforts of home were different, of course."

Coming back into Northeast, we pass one of these classic Bunker and Ellis yachts, the *Waterbed.* "She's all mahogany and teak," says David, "and the inside's almost all teak."

"I'd like to have been around Raymond more," David says. "I learned some of the boatbuilding skills, but I was never able to spend as much time as I'd like. He was quite a character and a skilled craftsman—you'd be talking to him, and all the time he'd be doing something that you wouldn't even notice. He'd go over and measure something, and keep working on it, talking all the while. Then he'd put it all together, and the bevels would be right, and everything fit right in like a shoe.

"In his late years, we were working on the *Sea Queen,* replacing some decking on her bow. Raymond was old, and he couldn't really see much or do much—I was running the tools for him. He wanted to match up the old screw holes with the ones we needed to drill in the new planking. He'd look things over and look them over again, then he'd say 'Let's put a hole right here.' I'd drill, and the bit would go right through into the old hole underneath. It was the same thing when he worked on a keel log—drilling for the propeller shaft to go through. He'd just look at it and drill it and the hole'd go right up through where it was supposed to be."

There's some of Raymond Bunker in his nephew. Throughout the trip out to Great Cranberry and back, David talked with me, answering questions and volunteering stories without once hesitating. All the while, he was dodging lobster buoys, watching for traffic, and keeping track of his boat and barge. Occasionally he'd step to the port side of the boat to look out the opposite side, without ever interrupting his conversation. When a couple of pleasure boats cut in front of the *Double B,* I remarked that with her barge, the boat must not be very maneuverable. "Oh, I'm used to her," was his simple answer.

Because David grew up on Great Cranberry and has been part of the business since he was old enough to amount to anything, lobsterboat and barge now appear to be extensions of himself.

KITTIWAKE II
A Family Pleasure Boat

Raymond Bunker and Ralph Ellis built at least sixty boats in the winters between 1946 and 1978, all but one of them of wood. About a third were finished as working lobsterboats, but today, Bunker and Ellis are best remembered for their pleasure boats. In establishing the tradition of lobster yachts, which now represent better than half of many builders' business, these two craftsmen set a high standard.

The bright (varnished) mahogany cabin sides that mark many of their boats are perhaps their best-known feature. Several of them have gracefully curved windshield sides with the canvas top of an open "picnic boat." They all have an elegance of line and pass through the water with ease. "Their design was very functional," says modern-day builder Mac Pettegrow. "They were shaped to get the engines down low in the boat, not to break any speed records. Raymond's boats go real clean, but they're not fast—just comfortable and seaworthy."

The largest boats Bunker and Ellis built were forty-four-footers, starting with *Kittiwake II* in 1964. She is open-topped, like several of the partners' pleasure boats, but she is unusual for being painted throughout. And, unlike most of the forty-twos and forty-fours, she has only a single engine. Jarvis Newman, Raymond Bunker's son-in-law and chronicler, says he personally prefers a single-engine boat in Maine's lobster-trap infested waters. "Twin screws are just like vacuum cleaners, sucking those buoys right up." Even if she's not typical in every detail, *Kittiwake II* is a fine example of the work done by Bunker and Ellis.

Just as she had good builders, this boat has certainly been fortunate in her people. She has had three owners since her launch: John Porter of Great Spruce Head Island; surveyor Giffy Full of Brooklin, Maine; and most recently, Doug Jacoby of Marblehead, Massachusetts. They all served her well, and she them. "I can't say enough good about the boat," states Giffy; Doug too, says he fell in love with her the first day he saw her. And John Porter's grandsons Aaron and Nathaniel ("Than") have affection, respect, and a little nostalgia in their voices when they talk about her.

James Porter, the father of *Kittiwake II*'s first owner, bought Great Spruce Head Island in East Penobscot Bay shortly before World War I. It has been the retreat for the still-growing Porter family ever since, and over the years, seven houses have been built there. John, James's youngest son and a schoolteacher, wanted to raise his family on a boat, but Trudy, his wife, didn't; Aaron and Than say that the island was the compromise.

"John was the one who kept the island going," says Aaron, "and *Kittiwake* was just a part of that." Although there were other boats on the island, it was *Kittiwake* that made nearly all the trips ashore. "John was willing to pick people up, and he enjoyed doing it, too—*Kittiwake* used to go back and forth for everyone," says Aaron. "She was the tender for the island. Camden was our base then; everyone did their banking and shopping and everything there, and it was quite a haul across the bay. But with *Kittiwake*, it didn't matter how many people were aboard."

Clearly the trip was an adventure for the young family members, who went along whenever they were allowed. "The crossing was a big deal," recalls Aaron. "And then we'd get to Camden, and everyone would sort of tear about. John would go up to Cappy's and have iced coffee while everyone else ran around. A boat that size was very comfortable, and there was plenty of room for a lot of people and a lot of groceries or big parts for the Caterpillar tractor— not that John wanted to have those greasy things on the teak," Aaron laughs.

"You weren't allowed to eat salted peanuts on the deck," says Than, "but of course, we all did."

"Especially John," says Aaron.

The special thing about *Kittiwake* for both Aaron and Than was her elegant simplicity. "She was very much an outdoor boat—her accommodations were ample but not opulent," says Than.

"Below, there was a little place to eat," Aaron remembers. "She had nice bunks, a head, and a nice galley, but there was no big saloon area as there is in so many yachts. I don't remember the lighting being very good, but we didn't do much below decks. The only important thing down there was the radio. John didn't have a transmitter ashore, just a receiver, which he listened to for an hour every night. If you were on the mainland and wanted to get in touch with him, you'd have to call the Camden Marine Operator during that hour. Then he'd run down, row out to *Kittiwake*, and answer the call. Or, if anyone on the island had to make a phone call, they'd have to go out to *Kittiwake*."

Than says that when he was fourteen or fifteen and forming an opinion about what a boat should be, *Kittiwake* was the example against which he compared other vessels. "She could do most anything I could ever imagine I'd want to do, yet she was so simple," he says. "She had a lot of room but not a lot of things that were going to break down." Than explains that everything about *Kittiwake* was easily maintained. For example, the boat was powered by

The lobster yacht **Kittiwake II** *is both beautiful and functional.*

a Detroit 6-71 diesel engine, which he describes as "ample, reliable, and pretty basic; everyone knew how to work on it." The engine box was bigger than it needed to be: "It was furniture, too," explains Than, "with a mattress on top that two people could stretch out on. Then when you opened it up, there was all kinds of space around the engine. It was really accessible."

Aaron remembers that there was once a bench aft, running across the stern end of the cockpit. "It was taken out almost immediately and never went back," he says. "It was in the barn for a while, and then on the big-house porch. It was a nicely varnished bench, well cushioned, but it was declared to be 'no good' in the boat," Aaron says. Maybe it proved difficult to drag the dinghy up over the stern with the bench there.

"Most Bunker and Ellis pleasure boats have a lot of brightwork and look very yachty," says Aaron. Not *Kittiwake II*. "Her paint was put on very well, but it was just paint." She looked equally at home in the fishing village of Stonington or in the ultra-rich summer community of Dark Harbor.

For three or four years after John retired, the Porters took *Kittiwake* down the inland waterway and spent the winters in Florida and the Bahamas. "People were funny about the boat down south," Trudy Porter says. "Of course, there they all have great plastic apartment houses for boats. They'd come over and look at her and say, 'Hmm, that's a great waste of space, all that open cockpit.' We enjoyed the comments. People from up north knew it was a Maine boat right away, though."

Then John and Trudy would bring *Kittiwake* back to Great Spruce Head in the summer. "We didn't hurry on the waterway," says Trudy. "We'd stop and visit people, or go to a bird sanctuary or flower plantation on the way back. If the azaleas were in, we'd stop and see the sights in St. Augustine or Charleston. We took plenty of time. Time is what you have. We didn't have to tie up at a marina every night; we anchored. She was a no-nonsense boat. We could be independent."

Giffy Full had long admired *Kittiwake II,* and when the time came for the Porters to sell her, Giffy didn't hesitate. "The first thing is that she's a handsome boat. If a boat doesn't look right, I don't want it," he says. "Second, she's a very practical boat. She has a big cockpit, she's a very good sea boat, the layout is logical, and I like the way she was built. She has very good storage, and everything is accessible—you can get at the diesel and service it without committing suicide.

"She carries a good practical engine, sized properly for the boat. At a reasonable speed, it's very efficient." Giffy admits that he looks at a boat differently from many people, who are in more of a hurry than he. "At nine knots, she uses two and a half gallons of fuel an hour, and that's driving two alternators and a refrigerator compressor besides. On two hundred gallons, you can run all the way to New York without worrying about fuel, then continue on to North Carolina.

"I added a mast and boom to lift the tender and to help my wife on and off—she had multiple sclerosis. And I put on a steadying sail—it was nice when the wind was blowing hard. I added electronics, too—radar, loran, a new depth sounder—and a refrigerator. To go to Florida without refrigeration is a pain. But I didn't change anything in the layout, I just added stuff. I did a lot to dress her up—I can't leave a boat well enough alone."

Every year, Giffy did more major reconstruction on *Kittiwake II*. He had the decks reefed out, caulked, and payed, which means that the seams between all the deck planks were cleaned, refilled, and resealed. He gave her a new stem, the substantial curved piece of wood that forms the leading edge of the bow. He also redid the house tops and replaced the canvas, teak trim, cushions, and drapes. "After all, she was twenty-five years old," he explains.

"We put a lot of mileage on her—we averaged probably five or six thousand miles a year," Giffy says. After that first winter, when he was working on her, Giffy and his wife took the *Kittiwake II* to Florida every winter, and they lived aboard her there for six years. "My wife loved the boat so much she'd refuse to get off it. People used to ask her to come and stay with them, but she'd say, 'If you want to see me, come and see me on the boat.'

"I only gave up *Kittiwake* because of our health problems," he says. "My main object was to sell her to someone who would take care of her. I had a paper trail of people who wanted to buy the boat—I could have gotten fifteen or twenty thousand dollars more than I did. People always say that, but it's true. I didn't know Doug Jacoby, but I had surveyed a schooner he'd owned, and I knew the care he took of his boats. That's why I sold her to him."

"I saw *Kittiwake* in Somes Sound a couple of years ago," says Aaron Porter. "We were in Valley Cove, and she came in and anchored. It was the Marblehead people—a man [Doug Jacoby] and his wife and a couple of kids, nine or ten years old. They tethered one of the kids astern in the peapod, and he rowed against the line for a half an hour, while the father and the other kid were fishing off the side, and the mother was sitting on the trunk cabin, leaning against the windshield, reading. It felt good to see the boat being used that way."

"I was just callin' to see if you was out."
"Yes, well I guess you'd call it I was out of my mind."
                              —VHF radio conversation

JARVIS NEWMAN
Focused on the Details

ike many who ended up building them, Jarvis Newman was introduced to lobsterboats by his forebears. His grandfather ran lobster smacks from Nova Scotia to Boston. And in 1942, Jarvis's father, then living in Connecticut, came home to Manset and went lobstering. Laurence Newman had just been told that he would only live another couple of years due to diabetes. "Now that he's eighty-nine, he questions that diagnosis," Jarvis jokes. "He was the most successful lobsterman on the coast. He had to work hard, though."

Jarvis himself went off to school, then worked in Ohio, Massachusetts, and finally New Hampshire. But he married Susan Bunker, a hometown girl and the daughter of boatbuilder Raymond Bunker. So, ten years after leaving Maine, he returned to work for Bob Hinckley in a fiberglass shop that many think turned out the finest production sailboats in the country.

Even then, Jarvis had entrepreneur in his makeup. A variety of projects led him finally to his own fiberglass boatbuilding venture, which produced dinghies at first, then Friendship sloops. One day, his father-in-law approached him. "Much as I hate fiberglass," said Bunker, "maybe you ought to build a powerboat."

It seemed like a good idea to Jarvis, and he made two molds, one for a twenty-five-foot Ray Hunt deep-V called the Surf Hunter. Jarvis only built a few of these boats, but the design was a good one and is still being produced in southern New England. His other mold was fashioned on a thirty-six-foot Bunker and Ellis lobsterboat, the *Irona*. He made the same deal with her owners as he'd made with the people who owned the *Old Baldy,* on which he had based his Friendship sloops: free winter storage and maintenance in exchange for permission to use the boat as the plug for a mold.

Jarvis was only the third person on the Maine coast to build fiberglass lobsterboats, and he did wonder who was going to buy a thirty-six-foot 'glass boat. But, he went ahead with the project nonetheless. In 1971, he sold the first hull to a fisherman from Gouldsboro, and the model took off. The early boats were all commercial models. "Once you sell a fisherman and he likes the boat, man, you've got something to sell to a pleasure boater. It's proven." Eighty-nine of these thirty-six-footers have been sold to date, about half for work and half for fun.

"If speed isn't a factor, the Newman 36 is the most comfortable small fiberglass boat on the market," says builder Mac Pettegrow, who ought to know; he's finished off a lot of them. "It's a nice sea boat. It rolls more than some, but the motion is pleasant; because the bilge is wider, it displaces more water."

The Newman 36 was one of the first fiberglass lobsterboats produced on the Maine coast.

The next project was a thirty-two-footer, which Jarvis and Ralph Stanley designed together in 1974. Three years later, Will Frost's grandson, Royal Lowell, designed a forty-six-footer for Jarvis. Like the models before it, this boat has been a success. Jarvis points at a 1980 *Yachting* magazine reprint relating to the forty-six. "They said that boat made twenty-eight knots with a single engine. I don't really think this hull does twenty-eight. Maybe twenty-five."

"I like the built-down style. It drops the engine down, it's stronger, and it's more seakindly. I know it's not quite as fast as the skeg boats." Interestingly, Jarvis doesn't like diesels. "People just want to hear that throatiness," he scoffs.

"It's not worth the hassle, and the noise, and the cost!"

Jarvis sold his boat business in 1980, but the models he originated are still being built.

He takes pride in the workmanship that characterized his boats; he and his crew turned out a hull a week, he says, and he never had more than three men working for him. He put cement in the bilges to keep the weight low and the boat stable. No sprayed layup for him, either; his boats were hand-built, layer by layer. Jarvis himself was always involved, laying up fiberglass and doing "fussy work" each night so the boat would be ready for the next stage the following day. But his business was hulls, and hulls alone.

"Let me do the messy part and put the engine in," he says, "and I'm happy to have other people do the wood." The only difference between a pleasure boat and a lobsterboat when they left Jarvis's shop was the placement of the engine: it was installed four feet farther aft in recreational models than in commercial vessels.

The Newman hulls were finished off all along the Maine coast and as far away as Maryland and New Jersey. Jarvis did complete two thirty-six-foot pleasure boats himself one winter, however, just to show people what could be done with his hulls. He attributes selling another hundred boats of various sizes to those two. Their details were right, he says. It is clear that in Jarvis's mind, it is the details that make or break the appearance—or strength or value or overall worth—of a boat. And the details are what he cares most about.

Jarvis brings out piles of photographs of each model, and admires—or chuckles scornfully at—each rendition. "Look at that house," he says. "Did you ever see anything so ugly?" or "Isn't that a nice one?" He has a very refined sense of the tiny features that make the difference between ordinary and beautiful. "Where you put the ports is super-important," he says. He shows pictures of boats with too many ports, ports that are too small, and ports that aren't lined up just to his liking.

According to Jarvis the design of the windshield is critical, too. Some boats have what he calls "crying windows," whose top and bottom edges both slant down toward the outside. Jarvis doesn't like those, usually. He shows me a photograph of a boat where the top edges of the windows are curved while the bottom edges are lined up straight. "That's good," he says. Of course, the front of the house in commercial lobsterboats is often flat, while pleasure-boat versions often show a pleasing curve. Visors, says Jarvis, make a difference, too.

But most important, he insists, is the boat's profile. A graceful sheerline is a given on a Newman, so Jarvis doesn't waste any more time discussing it. "I'm a nut on cabin sides," he says, "because that's what you see. People say, 'I want six-foot headroom and an icemaker,' but that's what kills a boat. If a guy wanted cabin sides three feet tall on a twenty-five-foot Friendship sloop, I'd tell him to go to Winnebago. I just wouldn't build the boat."

Jarvis says color can make all the difference. Sometimes, the trunk cabin is painted gray, emphasizing the sheerline while de-emphasizing the ports. Jarvis has two photographs of the same boat; in one, her hull is blue and her superstructure white, and in the other she is all white, except for her trunk cabin, which is gray. She looks good in the first picture, but elegant in the second.

The presence or lack of a trim piece along the top of the trunk cabin can make all the difference to the apparent proportion of cabin sides, says Jarvis. "It's essential. You're dead without it."

The Newman 32 clearly shows the influence of her co-designer, Ralph Stanley.

"The perfected boat," he says, "is Peter Godfrey's *Margaret.*" This boat was the first Newman 32 to come out of the mold, and she lives in Northeast Harbor. From the outside, she is plain, simple, clean. She looks like a lobsterboat. Her ports are just right, and the cabin roof is exactly the right length, its support post vertical. The trunk cabin is high enough and not too high. Below, she's bright and fancy, set up for comfortable weekending.

For all his interest in the looks of his boats, Jarvis doesn't forget that they were meant to go through the water. He takes pride in showing photographs of various Newmans at speed. They cut through the water easily, the bow wave making a clean curve and the stern wake negligible. One person who finished some of these boats put spray rails on the bow. Jarvis is still incensed. "He'd put spray rails on a bicycle! I never put spray rails on my boats. You don't need them."

Jarvis knows when things are right.

"How'd you do?"
"Nothin' famous. Oh, I had a couple traps about full. We'll eat tonight."
"Yeah, guess so. Worth haulin', I guess."

—VHF radio conversation

LYNN WESSEL
From Schoolteacher to Deckhand

When Lynn married Steve Wessel, he was lobstering from South Harpswell out of a Newman 36. She was teaching first grade in tiny, landlocked Pejepscot in a three-room schoolhouse that dated from the 1880s. Although she describes herself as an outdoor person, Lynn admits that she knew nothing about the ocean until she moved to the coast and started fishing with Steve at the end of the school year. "At first, I just went to catch some sun, but I got kind of bored," she says, "and I thought I might as well do something, be productive. So, I measured lobsters and then pegged them. I baited traps, too, when I had to."

She loved it and quickly learned what was important: Never, ever take a chance on keeping a "short," or illegal, lobster. "I'd been banding lobsters one day. Steve was pulling them out of the tank, when he looked at one and said 'This is a short!' Well, he took the bands off and pitched it overboard. I'd been told, 'When in doubt, throw it out,' but I guess I'd measured wrong. Steve was furious when he found a second one. . . ."

Subsequently, a year of teaching in a bigger school made Lynn question whether she wanted to continue in the classroom. She took a leave of absence. "Steve said he wasn't going to help me decide if I wanted to quit or not," she says. " 'You've got to make up your own mind,' he told me." The period when she went fishing during her leave from school was the first time Lynn had done just what she wanted to, and she liked the feeling. That was the year she and Steve were watching over construction of the *Misty Lynn,* a Newman 46 that Mac Pettegrow finished for the Wessels.

"We went to Southwest Harbor often—three days a week—and it was exciting to see the boat coming along. And the Pettegrows, Steve, and I all had such a good time together. It was almost a letdown when she was finished. All of a sudden, here was reality, and we had to pay for it. We ended up with two boats for a little while—that was kind of hairy, too. Steve wouldn't watch when the old one left; he tucked in behind an island so he wouldn't see her go.

Lynn and Steve Wessel christen their new lobsterboat.

"As it turned out, we put an awful lot more into the new boat than we needed—she was the fanciest lobsterboat of her time. Mac did a beautiful job with her. We could have lived aboard her, easily, and we planned to take her south and go cruising. We did go offshore, lobstering. But we both hated that, thank God!

"We thought it would be so romantic, so adventurous, to go offshore. Someone told me it was going to be really boring, and I said to myself, 'I guess you don't know me very well, if you think I'm going to be bored!' but that person was right. You steam, and you steam, and you steam, and you finally get there and put your traps in, and then what do you do? You wait. You set the gear twice, so you have to haul back at least twice. So you're sitting there a whole day. Steve had trawls [strings] of twenty-five traps, and hauling those is exhausting. Working the bay, everything's *bing, bing, bing, bing,* and when you're done with the *bing*s, you weigh up and you're finished. But out there, it's not like that. You've got the long steam home, and you're so tired when you get there, all you can do is sleep and buy groceries. Then out you go again."

Each trip lasted three or four days, maybe five. Lynn isn't sure. "It seemed like forever." She had signed on as cook but says, "I made a terrible cook—I don't like to cook anyhow; I'd much rather eat out. The crew knew more about cooking than I did or would let on to.

"And it's hard to cook when you're seasick. I'd never been sick before, but when we got to a certain point—Steve calls it the edge of bottom—the waves would be different. The motion of the boat was so different—oh, did I get sick! The first time I tried to fight it, and the second time I let her go, but it didn't help. Seasickness never bothered me inshore. Out there it's terrible—and it's

Designed by Royal Lowell, the Newman 46 was and is known for its speed and seakindliness.

worse for the cook. You're below all the time, and you're away from everybody, and then you get a little squeamish, and you've got all the smells. . . .

"We only went out to Georges Bank once—there was green water everywhere, smashing onto the windows. Our hair was standing on end. Steve said to me, 'Do you know, this is the pits?' 'Oh!' I said, 'I think so too!' I never would have said anything, because I'd signed on for whatever happened, but I was happy when he said that! And even now, when we go near the water and it's really howling out there, Steve says, 'Don't you wish you were on your way to Georges?' Oh, sure!

"David—Steve's brother—loved it offshore. The rougher it was, the better. He *tried* to bury the bow! I think there's some escapism in fishing off-shore—it's terribly hard work, but the guys out there don't have to face the mundane things on shore, like getting the groceries and taking the kids to the doctor. It's dangerous out there. I didn't know it until later, but you don't ice up offshore, because you're in the Gulf Stream. Coming back in, that's when you ice up; you get so top-heavy, it's really dangerous. But David and his crew loved the wild experience. It's different personalities—those people love the adventure. Steve and I are basically homebodies, we like to stay home. But David finally gave it up, too—it's too hard with a family."

After he stopped going offshore, Steve fished for lobster along the coast for three more years. Lynn admits she's biased but says her husband is a good fisherman. And it turned out that the big *Misty Lynn* worked well inshore. "He'd be out when nobody else could go out. He did extremely well that way. There was one November—as bad a November as I remember—when he really didn't miss many days. But all the other boats were tied up at the dock."

Off South Harpswell, in Casco Bay, lobstermen fish in trawls, six to fif-teen traps on each warp, with a buoy on each end. After he moved back inshore, Steve fished fifteen-trap trawls. At one point, he was working as many as 3,000 traps, but then he backed off and found he got just as many pounds of lobster by setting fewer traps and paying better attention to them. "He liked to keep a two-night set," says Lynn. "Sometimes he and another boat would be hauling side-by-side, each one trying to be faster than the other. He had an incredibly fast crew.

"But by December, when the traps would come up for the winter, Steve would be hurting," notes Lynn. "He had bursitis, first in his right shoulder and then in his left, and now he's got bad veins in one leg, the one he braced against most of the time. He worked so hard, so long, he burned himself out," she says.

"Steve came home one day from lobstering and said, 'I guess I'll start a brokerage.' 'Oh good,' I said. 'I know how to type. . . .'" The Wessels didn't know anything about boat brokerage, but, says Lynn, "Steve had fished so long, he certainly knew about boats, and I knew more than I thought I did, because I'd been on the boat with him and because we'd spent so much time with Mac when he was building the *Misty Lynn*." The first boat they sold was for a friend; with the commission, they bought a copier, and the business went on from there. And when summer came and Steve decided to go back to fishing, Lynn guessed she could do the brokerage alone. "As long as you don't lie to people, they don't care if you don't know everything," she says.

Lynn tells of another boat broker who ran a huge advertising campaign in the commercial-fishing publications for a couple of years, fouled up deals for other brokers, and ended up running off with people's deposits. "That guy did more damage—fishermen are avoiding brokers now. And if you don't catch a fisherman when he's hot, you've lost him," says Lynn. "When they get bored—

usually around January 15, when Christmas is over, they've got their mending done, and they're bored—then they want a new boat, and they want it *now*.

"Most of them know what they want, or which three or four models they'd consider, and which three or four they definitely wouldn't want. And they have engines they want or don't want—that's often geographical. Steve always tells people to put in the engine they'll get the best service on, and he says the same for electronics.

"Steve's having been a fisherman has given him an edge in the business. At first, he worried that he wouldn't be as good as a broker because he wasn't as polished as some, but it's worked for him, I believe. He'll wear his blue jeans most anywhere; 'I'm not going to stand there and have the fishermen think that I see myself as better than they are,' he says.

"That's why I have been quite lucky in dealing with fishermen, because I understand them," Lynn says. "For instance, I don't ask a fisherman to stay at the dock just because someone might come look at his boat, because too often the buyer doesn't show up. That would mean a lost day's pay for the fisherman. And we don't get the fishermen to sign a contract—I'd rather go on a handshake."

And so, of course, would they.

"The absolutely lovely characteristic of a lobsterboat is the speed-to-rpm curve. For each application of throttle, you get a commensurate increase in speed.
—Spencer Lincoln, Brooklin

SPENCER LINCOLN
Lobsterboat Designer

Mac Pettegrow says of Spencer Lincoln, "For fiberglass, he's on the top of the heap. More of his models are successful than not, and he's had more of them produced than anyone else. And, he's a good guy."

I had a terrible time convincing Spencer to talk with me. I called him up in February. He said he doesn't like to do interviews on the phone: "It's so impersonal." But it wasn't convenient for him to get together. He said I could call in another couple of weeks.

I tried that. It didn't work. He was going surfing in Hawaii, he said. "Call in a couple of months," he suggested. I called in June. "You're not going to give up, are you?" he asked. I told him no, I wasn't. I suggested that perhaps we could just try it on the phone. "How long will it take?" he asked.

"Well, we could start with two or three minutes, and see what happens."

"OK," he said reluctantly. "What do you want to know?"

I asked some general question about lobsterboat design.

"That's not where I'd begin," he said, and proceeded to talk with only minor prodding for forty-five minutes.

"I'm an oddball in the whole organization," Spencer says. "I wasn't lobstering with my father from the age of five. I grew up looking at lobsterboats, but not spending eighteen hours a day in them." He can't say how many different models he is responsible for, but he knows he always wanted to design boats. "Boats relate to the water, and the water is where it's at. You start from the water. The best designs are the ones that address how well the boat goes through the water, irrespective of speed."

71

Spencer started out drawing houses, he says, and got within one course of finishing a degree in architecture. "They always told me the value of an education was the education, not the degree, so I took them at their word." He doesn't think much of the training he received; he says it didn't teach him about actually putting anything together. "It was from the top down, and not the bottom up." But he got lucky, he says, and has been designing boats for twenty years now. He guesses that 75 percent of his designs are lobsterboat-style hulls. He enjoys the challenge. "The part of the boat underneath the water is the most important—I love to fool around with it."

Spencer Lincoln

BRIAN ROBBINS

Spencer says that the lower maintenance required by fiberglass makes it a better material than wood for commercial fishing boats, but because each molded 'glass hull is produced in quantity, the design criteria have changed. "In the old days, it used to be you could custom build, thanks to the material: wood. A sharp builder could ascertain what the use for the boat would be, and adjust the shape or dimensions accordingly. Now, one design has to suit a variety of purposes. One in ten boats is perfect for its job, perhaps, and the rest are compromises. But," he says, "the fun of this business is to make a hull which is adaptable."

Two of Spencer's earlier models, both very successful, are the BHM 31 and the Duffy 35. Developed in the late 1970s and early '80s, these boats were among the first designed specifically for the lightweight, high-powered marine diesels then coming on the market. Both boats are broader and have straighter bottoms than their predecessors. "The old-fashioned, slow lobsterboat has a lot of rocker, as suits a displacement hull," Spencer explains, describing a convex curve in the bottom, running from bow to stern. "It allows the water to rise at the bow, fall in the middle, and rise again as it approaches the transom. That's appropriate at ten to twelve knots, but not at twenty. Today's lobsterboat is a semi-planing boat." He describes both the Duffy 35 and the BHM 31 as "a nice marriage of power plant and hull; they floated well, ran well, and ran at a good speed for the horsepower."

The Duffy 35 makes a handsome, comfortable lobster yacht.

Although Spencer designed these two boats with some of the same goals in mind, they are very different from each other. "That was in response to the company owners. One [Duffy] wanted a lean, fast, fighting machine, and the other [Flye Point Marine] wanted the biggest little boat in the bay, with the largest amount of cubic feet in the hull." The BHM 31 is described by its designer as "a heck of a tub, but a very useful boat."

Each boat attracted its own following. The Duffy 35 is well accepted both commercially and in the pleasure market. It is available in two forms, one with a low sheer and the other with a rail that is some six inches higher. "As a lobsterboat," Spencer says, "it'll weigh about 12,000 pounds, and as a pleasure boat it will be closer to 16,000. It can accommodate both weights fairly easily."

Although the BHM 31 is four feet shorter, it has the same twenty feet of cockpit as the Duffy 35. Mac Pettegrow calls it a seagoing pickup truck.

Even today, the Duffy 35 and the BHM 31 remain best sellers, according to Kent Lawson of Atlantic Boat Company, which now manufactures both. He notes, however, that a couple of larger, more recent models—also Spencer's designs—are coming on strong. Commercial fishing-boat broker Lynn Wessel says she can't get enough of either the 35 or the 31. Despite the age of their designs, both boats are always in demand.

Chunky and blunt-nosed, the BHM 31 is a versatile hull capable of carrying a lot of weight.

Part of the reason for the enduring popularity of these models lies in the easy running characteristics to which Spencer continually refers when he talks about lobsterboat hulls. He explains that a semi-planing lobsterboat has a constant speed-to-rpm curve. "When you put the gear ahead, you go four or five knots; then, for each application of throttle, you get a commensurate increase in speed. There is no huge 'step' the way there is on a planing boat. For every 200-rpm increase in engine speed, you may get, say, a two-knot increase in boat speed.

"That makes the lobsterboat unlike a planing boat, and lovely in its own regard," says Spencer. "I would call a good lobsterboat sort of a glider, with a very versatile speed-to-rpm curve. There are advantages to that. In many instances, you can't go faster than twelve knots; when you get out in a heavy breeze and the sea has kicked up, you don't want to go twenty. Actually, the boat can take it, but the human beings won't.

"There's a relationship between weight and horsepower, and there are some places in the speed curve where the lobsterboat hull will go easily at low cost. But if you increase speed just one knot, fuel consumption goes up significantly." Spencer gives as an example a big, heavy pleasure boat, one he admits is on the outer edge of being defined as a lobster yacht. This vessel burns thirty gallons per hour at seventeen knots, but forty gallons per hour at eighteen knots.

"There are 'sweet spots' for every boat—an rpm at which the engine feels good—but it's dependent upon the weight," says Spencer. He quotes a manufacturer down east who makes a telling statement about his own 36-footer, "With an engine weight over 2,500 pounds, the boat don't feel so good."

Spencer recently designed a new model called the Northern Bay 36. "She ran 20.5 knots with 260 horsepower at 14,000 pounds. That's a little more performance than some," he says, his voice betraying his pleasure. The first racing done by this model demonstrates Spencer's understatement. In 1997, Andy Gove's *Uncle's UFO* ran faster than any diesel-powered lobsterboat had before in competition, and she was dueling all season with the gas-powered race boats.

The workboat version of the original Duffy 35 was intended to be "a lean, fast fighting machine."

"I'm trying for a slightly more advanced hull. It has a little less forefoot [the part of the bow at the stem, below the waterline], and there's less planing angle—the bow doesn't have to come up so high to plane the boat." He places a lot of importance on the buttocks, the lines that would be defined if you sliced the hull lengthwise into a series of longitudinal sections. Spencer says these lines determine the running character of the boat in semi-planing mode.

"I can push and pull and tug to change the shape of the underbody," he says. "Water is very dense—sixty-four pounds per cubic foot—so with a very small change in volume below the waterline, I can change how the boat floats a heck of a lot. I can fool with volumes within the semi-built-down area versus the buttocks, and get the buttocks close to the surface of the water, so they'll break clear easier."

Spencer emphasizes that all boat designers have their own approach and their own overall view. While they may talk about particular details, the overall image they have of their boat is even more important. "You just can't take things in isolation," he says.

Spencer tells me that he is finishing a small lobster yacht for himself, to add to his eclectic flotilla. The boat is based on the Webco 22 hull, which he designed years ago for a company in East Blue Hill. It's a model he's pleased with, because it offers boating to people who might not be able to afford it otherwise. "I'd like to have a bumper sticker that says 'Put the middle class back in boating,'" he says. "We read too many magazine articles, that's the trouble. For instance, if you think you've got to have ten coats of varnish before you can go out, you're going to be separated from the water by a $6,000 varnish bill."

The Webco 22 is unusual in that it has a hard chine, or corner, molded into the fiberglass hull at the bilges, a "spray knocker," Spencer calls it. "When you get a boat speed of more than twenty knots, you want something to knock the spray down. The boat's drier and more stable because of it." Why isn't this feature more common? "You can approach lobsterboats from a variety of directions," says Spencer. "If you look at this one with a traditional eye, the older boats don't have the spray knocker, and therefore the eye might be offended. But that chine does serve a useful purpose at higher speeds.

"You can enter the design process from a variety of different perspectives—primarily looks or performance—and come up with a different result. You just have to live with that result."

THE YOUNG BROTHERS
Building Family Pride

Corea is the last village on the Schoodic peninsula, and the Young Brothers shop is out on the most distant point. Arvid Young says he has lost two wives due to living out there; just a little way up the hill, it's usually sunny and warm but out where he lives and works, it's thick-a-fog. His first wife stood it for twenty-five years. His second wife didn't last nearly so long. Arvid ("Vid"); his twin brother, Arvin ("Vin"); and their older brother, Colby, are the seventh generation of the Young family to live in Corea, and they have been building fiberglass lobsterboats there for twenty years.

The twins joined the Coast Guard in 1958 and had served ten years when it appeared they'd be sent to Vietnam. It was time to leave the service. "But you're a career sailor," Vid's executive officer said to him.

"Watch my smoke," said Vid. "It'll be headed east to Corea."

Returning home, Vin and Vid joined their father, their brother, and most of the other men of Corea fishing for lobsters. One winter, they bought three 'glass hulls and finished them. Arvid didn't like how his handled, so he sold her. "That was pretty easy," he says. "No one was building skeg boats in 'glass then, so we got to wondering if we couldn't do it." The Youngs all prefer the traditional Jonesport–Beals Island design.

"A skeg boat is faster," says Vid.

Colby adds, "And a built-down boat has a natural roll built right into her."

Arvid takes over again. "If you're hauling north and south, like here, and the tide runs east and west, you particularly don't want a boat that rolls. A boat's most treacherous in her own wake. If you get her loaded up and make a turn around a buoy, you can roll traps right out of her. The more weight you

77

put on a skeg boat, the more steady she becomes. I was down to Bar Harbor one day, and Ronald Rich—he was a good wooden-boat builder out in Southwest Harbor—said, 'My boat is like sailing with a fifty-five-gallon drum underneath you in the water. Yours runs right over the water.'"

Colby adds, "They used to tell me there was more wood in a built-down boat. But it'll rot just as quickly, won't it?"

"One time," says Arvid, "I was hauling traps in a semi-built-down boat, and by the time I was half-filled with traps, I was going careful. I didn't want to lose them traps. But my brother there, in a skeg boat, he was just slapping traps on. 'How can you do that?' I asked him, but it was just because he was in a skeg boat."

Colby laughs. "Yeah, I rolled seventeen traps off a built-down boat one day. They still set there, right out back of Sally's Island rocks."

That first winter, the Youngs took a thirty-eight-foot Beals boat they liked the looks of and cleaned her up to use as a plug for their mold. "She'd been in the ice three winters and needed a lot of fairing up," says Vid. "We started taking her gear off in November and went right at her with the wet sandpaper. We sanded until the blood would come right through from our fingers, trying to get her somewhere near smooth. We were working seven days a week, ten or twelve hours a day, for seven weeks. We wouldn't want to do it now."

"Couldn't do it now," Colby says.

"A lot of the time, we'd shake our heads and wonder just what we were up to. But we took the first boat out of that mold on a Saturday, and that day we sold six more. We looked at each other and decided we had to fish or cut bait. So we went into the boatbuilding business." Young Brothers has always been a family operation, and there's a little sadness in Arvid's voice as he explains that his dad never got to see it. The elder Young died just a couple of months before they started up. "Boatbuilding was in our family—there were plenty of boatbuilders and ship's carpenters," says Vid. "Course, no one had any schooling in it, but they knew their business. Three of our great-uncles were master carpenters. My father had the attitude that he couldn't whittle a button for a shithouse door, but he knew what it was supposed to look like when it was done."

The respect that Vid has for his family is clear. "Colby is mechanically inclined. He's probably the most talented man on the coast when it comes to mechanics and hydraulics and that kind of thing. When we got started, pot haulers and power steering were just coming in, and he taught us." Their mother was in the company until recently, too. "She'd been teaching school," says Vid, "but we could offer her more money, working in the office. Now she's seventy-four and real active. She still rides her bicycle, and she's been playing the organ here at the church since 1945. She's always busy."

The Youngs built more than thirty boats from their first mold. "The original buyer of the last one is still sailing her, in Long Island," Vid reports.

They've made seven more molds since, from thirty to forty-five feet, always from a new plug and all designed by Ernest Libby Jr. of Beals Island. "He's a great innovator," Vid says. "If he built two boats and one outsailed the other, he'd find out why. He's got a great eye. He only went through eighth grade, but he knows, and he's a Class-A gentleman. Of course, if you ask him a question, you'd better want the answer, because he'll tell you."

Young Brothers does all its own tooling work, so it takes a long time to start up a new line. First they build a wooden plug, right side up, then they turn it over and make the mold around it. "It took eleven months from the start till we were ready for production on the 42," says Arvid. To date, they've turned

Arvin, Colby, and Arvid Young take a break inside the split mold for one of their lobsterboat hulls.

out around four hundred boats. "All but three of them are still alive," says Vid. "One burned in a finish shop just before launch, and two sunk, one in North Carolina and one just off here. The fellow in North Carolina will be back. He called and said he's working for someone else now, and he doesn't really like that."

The boats have faced plenty. Arvid shows me a photo of a thirty-three-footer called the *Sea Scorpion*, built for a Bermuda fisherman. "She left here and went to Newport, Rhode Island," he explains. "She had bladders on deck for extra fuel, because it's a six-hundred-mile run out to Bermuda from there. There were three guys on board, and they got hit by a surprise storm. They had winds of eighty and eighty-five miles per hour, along with thirty-five- and forty-foot seas or better." Arvid says the boat was side-to the storm and would rise to the top of a wave, fall thirty feet, rise to a another crest, then fall thirty feet again—for hours on end.

"An ocean liner came into Bermuda with a lifeboat all stove up, and everyone had given up on the *Scorpion*. But, she came trudging in, a day and a half late. The only damage was in the wiring conduit running to the flybridge. It was a squared box with the trim strips hot-glued on, because we didn't want to use screws for fear of hitting the wires. Those strips broke loose where all three of them was hanging on for their lives.

" 'We swore a lot, we cried a lot, and we prayed a lot,' the men told us. 'Thank God for Young Brothers boat.' I think the extra weight of the bladder bags of fuel is what saved her," Arvid says.

The skeg-built, Beals Island–style hull of the Young Brothers 38 makes her a fast, stable platform.

At present, the Young Brothers shop runs four ten-hour days; there's a crew of six on the floor and two in the office. "If the fellows in the mold room want to take a few extra smoke breaks, I don't say anything to them," says Vid. "That's hard work. Finding a crew hasn't been that difficult, though Corea's not like Southwest Harbor or Beals, where there've always been a lot of boat-builders. Fourteen of our ex-employees are building yachts at Hinckley, and Hinckley says we're the best school they've got."

There was a time—in the 1980s—when twenty-five people were work-ing at Young Brothers. That was before passage of the so-called luxury tax that hurt so many boatbuilders. "I read that before that tax, there were nine good sailboat builders just in the state of New Jersey. And now there's only three left," says Vid. "Our own senator, George Mitchell, down there in Washington, had control over what bills came out onto the floor, and he kept saying we'd get that tax taken off. But by the time the bill got to the floor, they'd amended it so many times and added so much onto it, it took them forever to get the tax off."

Asked if he worries about the market now, Arvid laughs. "Not one little bit." If you order a Young Brothers boat today, it'll be a year and a half before they can deliver it. But they're not rushing to add on more men again, although they had plans drawn up for a two-hundred-foot addition to the shop. In fact, they had the loans in line to build it a while back. "We were going to start on a Monday," Vid says, "and on Friday, we just looked at each other and said, 'What are we doing?' and canceled the whole works. We don't need to be any bigger."

Arvid takes pride that the harbor at Corea has more Young Brothers lobsterboats than anything else. "We've built a lot of them for people we all grew up with. Some builders can't sell a boat around home—there's too many little squabbles, or something. In Cutler, twelve out of fifteen boats are ours. But we can't get one into Swan's Island, I don't know why that is. It's all Duffy, there. We've built for fathers and sons, and for brothers. We have just two in Canada, but we've heard more from the Canadians than we used to." Vid says a Canadian was in the other day, a fellow who runs thirty miles a day, crabbing.

"You trying to tell me a ten- or twelve-mile-an-hour boat won't cut it?" Arvid asked him.

"That's right," the Canadian said.

"Then you can't have any little 250-horsepower motor, you know."

"All right, what about that?" the Canadian asked, pointing to a photograph of a speeding boat on the office wall.

"She's got 600 horsepower," Arvid told him. The Canadian was impressed. "Well," Arvid said, "if you're going to take a fourteen-ton boat and push it over the ocean, you aren't going to do it with a mustard paddle."

In addition to quantum increases in engine output, there have been many other changes in boatbuilding since the Young brothers started turning out 'glass boats. Arvid describes the first time he saw a chopper-gun demonstrated. These devices simultaneously chop multi-strand fiberglass "string" into short lengths, wet the fibers with resin, and blow them into a mold—forming a thin layer—all at very high speed. When the Young brothers agreed to try one, they turned a skiff upside down as a plug and laid up one side with rolled mat, by hand. Then the company representative did the other half of the boat with a chopper gun. "It makes our side look archaic, don't it?" the brothers agreed.

Arvid explains in more detail how the gun works. "All it does is allow you to make your own mat. It measures very minutely, so you have a perfect blend of catalyst and resin. And when the mixture hits the mold, 90 percent of the air is gone. After we go over it with metal rollers, 99 percent of the air is gone. And when you see a thin spot, you can just *pssst*, hit the trigger again."

Vid says, however, that Young Brothers now uses the chopper gun only to spray a resin-rich layer (called the skin coat) behind the gelcoat that goes into the mold first. It's a proven method of preventing the blistering that can affect a fiberglass hull if it isn't built right. Vid goes on to explain that the 'glass fabric they lay up in today's hulls is already bonded to a layer of mat, so they don't need to use the chopper gun as much. "The strength is in the 'glass," says Vid, "there's no strength in the resin. Where the ratio of resin to glass used to be 60:40, it's now 50:50 or better."

There have been other developments, as well. "We stopped using fiberglass rudders, though they'd last a fisherman forever," says Vid. "But on the pleasure boats, they usually have automatic pilots, and those make so many corrections, the 'glass rudders cracked. So now we use stainless steel.

"We get as much made locally or in Maine as we possibly can," Vid explains. "The pot haulers and power steering come from National Marine in Tenants Harbor. Castings come from Waterline Marine in East Blue Hill.

"We used to buy a lift of plywood a month, but now we've gone to molded fiberglass tops. We still use plywood in the bulkheads and the flooring, but we use all foam core—with 'glass on both sides—in the decks and in the sides of the trunk and house. Another thing that's almost nonexistent in here now is paint. The bottom is gelcoat, left bare, and every six or eight weeks you haul her out and hit her with Clorox. In this cold water, that's all you need. Of course, west of here—in New York and so forth—they do paint the bottoms.

"When we started, we hardly ever put diesel in a lobsterboat," says Vid. "Now they're all diesel. It's much more efficient, and there's less fire hazard. And, we use a wet [water-cooled] exhaust in 99 percent of our boats, so you don't have to worry about that hot pipe going up through the house." Arvid describes powering a thirty-eight-foot tuna boat they built with a six-cylinder (in-line), 650-horsepower Mack diesel. "Those engines develop tremendous torque," he says. "The boat's got a 1:1 ratio gear, turning a 24-inch by 31-inch, six-bladed propeller." Arvid says that in the early days, the old 38-footers were typically set up with a 320-horsepower, low-compression Oldsmobile engine with a 2:1 gear and a 22-inch by 20-inch, four-bladed propeller.

Speed is obviously important to the Young brothers. There are photographs of racing lobsterboats all over Arvid's office, and the shelves on three walls are nearly filled with trophies. He talks about how much they learned from racing—about propellers and hull shape and so on—but as he continues, the conversation turns more toward boats that proved themselves outside of formal racing. Arvid says that at one time, his dad held the record for the fastest time on the return trip from a certain buoy visible from Vid's window.

Still, the old racing memories are very much alive. Perhaps the most famous Young Brothers boat ever was Arvid's original *Sopwith Camel*, which was named by fellow boatbuilder and racing enthusiast Glenn Holland. His race boat is named the *Red Baron*. And the *Sopwith Camel*'s successor, the *Camel II*, was even faster. Vid says she made sixty-four miles per hour one time.

I ask him how it feels to do that.

"The water's quite hard. Wicked hard. Even at fifty miles an hour it's wicked hard," Arvid answers.

But speed and racing aren't the only priorities at Young Brothers. All three Youngs say honesty is important to them. Colby describes a conversation with a prospective buyer:

"How will I know if I send you so-many thousand dollars that you'll send me a boat?" asked the customer

"Because I say so," Colby told him.

"We build boats on a handshake," Arvid says with pride. He describes negotiating with a local millionaire summer resident. " 'Now I'm on a budget just like you're on a budget,' he told me. 'The only difference is the intervals.' But we worked out a plan, and we all kept to it."

Like so many boatbuilders, Arvid cites the people he's met as his favorite aspect of the business. "People are everything, aren't they?"

"We've met some corkers," Colby says, "and we've met some bastards too," but neither Young talks about those.

"We've sold boats to Green Harbor," says Arvid, "or York, or places like that, and the people there always say, 'Stop in if you have a chance.' Of course, none of us ever has because we're so busy. But Colby is our delivery man—if a boat has to be taken somewhere, he takes it."

Colby speaks again. "If I have to go anywhere like New York, I always make a phone call to a customer in Gloucester [Massachusetts], and there's usually a six-pack and a steak ready for me when I get there."

"When we do get around anyplace, we get treated like royalty," Arvid says.

But for all the friends they've made and races they've won, perhaps it's the boats themselves that, in the end, mean the most to the Youngs. Passing through the shop, Arvid stops to gently stroke the bow of a thirty-three-footer nearing completion in the shop. "Some boat," he says quietly.

*"It's just like Christmas, haulin' traps—you never
know what you're gonna get."*

—Gweeka Williams

Seining Aboard the
QUEEN D'ANNA

In 1979, Avery Kelley of Beals Island was looking
for a boat. "I'd had a good summer seining herring the year before, and then
that summer was real good. I was ready for a new boat." He wanted a big one,
forty-five feet, and he wanted it wide; he was going to seine fish offshore.

Purse seining demands a lot of a boat: It must bear the weight of a big net
with which to surround a large school of fish; typically, it must also carry a
good-sized skiff to tow the net in the opposite direction to close the circle; and
it must be stable when the fish-filled net is drawn to the side of the boat by a
heavy hydraulic winch mounted aloft, on a boom.

Avery looked around at every builder's models. "Young Brothers' wasn't
building their forty-five when I started looking, but they was talkin' about it.
Jarvis Newman had that forty-six-footer, but she was only fifteen feet wide and
thirteen feet at the stern. Jock Williams had a forty-four-footer, but that boat
was just twelve feet at the stern. The Youngs said they was going to build a
forty-five-footer that would be fourteen feet wide with a thirteen-foot stern. I
said to them, 'If you got to compete, you got to get it wider.' But they wasn't
going to give.

"So, I finally decided the only thing I could do was go to Canada," says
Avery, "which I didn't want to do. We headed out, but when we got to where
you'd turn off to Corea, we went there. We walked through the door, and there
they was with the biggest smiles on their faces.

" 'You talked to Nernie?' they asked—their designer is Ernest Libby Jr.,
and that's his nickname.

" 'Nope,' I says. Well, they had a model of my boat. 'How wide is she?' I asked.

" 'Fifteen,' they told me.

" 'How long?'

" 'Forty-five.'

" 'How wide at the stern?'

" 'Fourteen.'

" 'Well, how much money you got to have for that boat right now?' I asked, and that's how the boat got started.

"They haven't really sold too many. It's just a little bit big for fishing lobsters inside. It is a big, big boat, with big living quarters." He shows a photo of the *Queen D'Anna* loaded nearly to the rail, floating deep in the water. "That's 32,000 pounds of fish there," Avery says. "She's lugged pretty well."

Avery describes a seining trip: "We used to sail about five in the afternoon, four of us altogether, at least. We'd steam from here, probably as far as Roque Bluffs; we've always fished there. We'd eat our supper—this would be in the month of July, when the fish start runnin'. The days would be long; it wouldn't get dark before nine." Herring seining, he explains, is done at night, when the fish rise to the surface or move into shallow water.

"We had a big paper recorder that showed the schools of fish on it when they was deep," says Avery. "It ran by sonar, and if the fish was really thin, we'd call it peppery; if they was thick, it'd blacken in. For then, 1979, it was modern electronics." But the human eye, he says, also played an important role in finding the herring. "When it gets dark out, the water starts to fire," Avery explains. "They always used to say it was phosphorus, but really it was many trillions of plankton—this is what people smarter'n me tell me. If fish disturb it, it lights up like fireflies, that's how I call it. So we'd put two men on the bow to look for the water firin', showin' there's fish.

"If we found fish, we could go right into a cove, back into the land, and send a fellow ashore with a rowboat and the twine. Then we'd scoot right out of there trying to stay on the outside of them. Sometimes we'd send an outboard in. We only had just a short period of time—it seemed that the fish stayed on shore to feed good only till about midnight, and they left when the tide left the cove. Every night, the tide would be an hour later, so we had an hour longer. But if the fish was feedy, they'd be no good for cannin'—it blows the guts out of them. Just like when you go in the hospital, they don't want you full of food.

"Well, if there wasn't nothin' at Johnsons Cove, we'd go to Macks Cove—Cow Point we called it. One night we got $50,000 worth in Macks Cove. It took three days to bail them out. You could keep them things penned in for months, though they'll get thin. Two or three weeks would actually make a better packing fish, a little thinner.

"Once you've shut them in, you call the factory—most generally from Rockland they was, then—and they'd come out and load up. It'd take them seven hours to get to us." Would the seine crew sleep while they were waiting? "Well, you might sleep—we could go 'bout three days, and then our heads would kinda thump." Avery admits that as owner of the boat, his responsibility was greater, and sleep came harder. "I had so much to worry about—the twine was kinda old, and you got to keep nylon out of the sun, and so on. . . .

"The sardine carrier comes, and they put their suction hose down in the net and suck them out. It's a vacuum pump, run by hydraulics. Sucks in water, fish, and scales. There's a wire box that separates the herring—with a smaller mesh for the scales—then the water runs on out. So, fish come out one side,

The fifteen-foot beam of the Queen D'Anna *is extreme for a lobsterboat hull that's forty-five feet long.*

scales another, and water another." Fish scales were in demand for use in making fingernail polish, Avery says. "When the carrier's all loaded up, he takes off for the cannery, and you take your gear up or wait for fish to come in. That time in Macks Cove, we loaded the *Jacob Pike* several times, the *Delca,* the *Lawrence Wayne* more than once, the *Irma,* and the *Gary Ellen.*"

In the early days of Maine's herring fishery, the fish were taken primarily in weirs—essentially net-lined stockades of closely spaced poles driven into the bottom just offshore. Only later did fishermen learn the trick of using nets to close off, or "stop," the coves into which the herring move at night. Avery says his grandfather was one of the first stop-seiners. "Before that it was all weirs, and if the fish didn't come you didn't get nothin'. But a seiner could go where the fish were. There was always a cycle of herring along the Maine coast—years when they'd come to shore and some when they wouldn't. Then we went to planes [spotter aircraft], and that took the guesswork out. You could circle the fish in the middle of the bay, get them every night."

But now there are only five Maine canneries, laments Avery, and they have their own boats. There's no market for an independent fisherman's herring except as lobster bait, and that's not even an option down east, where the lobstermen don't want it. The *Queen D'Anna* isn't seining any more. "I've done everything with her," Avery says with pride. He shows another picture. "She's doing twenty knots there, with 300 horsepower. I've done shrimpin' and fish draggin'; I've dragged scallops, purse seined, and run fish food and fish down to the salmon pens. I've run bait, too—she's got a hold below decks that takes 15,000 pounds of fish, and I've had as high as 32,000 in her.

"I was even in the lobster haulin' contest over to Grand Manan [Canada], years ago. You left the dock, sailed out, hauled five traps, and sailed back while they timed you. They beat me out, and some wanted me to protest, because I only had one man aboard and they had three. But I said no, I was a guest in their country, and it was just an honor to be there. I'd never hauled traps with the *Queen* before, neither; I'd only just put the arm [hauling davit] on. I have the ribbon here they give me. Their people there have been some good to me over the years. They're my kind of fishermen, up there in Grand Manan." Avery, it seems, has friends all up and down the coast.

"There was one time, we had engine problems. It was the middle of the winter, probably the middle of January. The cold weather had really set in. That morning, it blew a gale of wind, comin' in northeasterly, probably around fifty, and the temperature hung around zero. Dwight Carver towed the *Queen D'Anna* to Stonington with a thirty-six-foot Calvin boat. I think it was about eleven below when we headed out towin' early in the mornin'. It was rough, and the sea smoke kept up all day, and we never saw the *Queen D'Anna* behind us till two o'clock in the afternoon, in York Narrows. We knew we hadn't lost her, it was pullin' real hard. You'd known the minute you lost her, but he didn't have radar on that boat, just loran, it'd been quite a job to find her if we'd lost her. Wasn't that a cold day."

This winter, Avery's youngest son is dragging for urchins with the *Queen D'Anna*. Derrick Kelley likes being his own boss, and Avery is happy not to be doing such hard work. "The older I get, the less I want to be on the ocean," he says. "I've had this winter off, and I've never felt better in my life."

Still, Avery understands that older men sometimes get the urge to go out again. One night, years ago, he was getting ready to sail on a quick trip. An elderly friend was visiting and, says Avery, "kind of hangin' around. I just knew he wanted to come with us." He called the man's wife to say her husband was going along so she wouldn't worry about him.

" 'You do what you want with him,' she says. 'Keep him if you want.' So we went out—him and me and my two boys—and we shut fish off. That old man was some excited."

Avery says he would like to catch one more herring himself before he dies. "If I see one more shut-off, I'll be happy. Last year we had those cussed kyacks, what we call sawbellies. They're between an alewife and a herring—if you run your finger along their belly it'll cut you. It looks so much like a herring from the top, it's a job to tell the difference. We got all these fish shut off last year, and I kinda smelled a rat before I dipped them. It was 100 percent kyacks. Never seen anything like it before. You might get a five-gallon pail of them in a hundred hogsheads, normally.

"But fishing is cycles, always has been."

DICK PULSIFER
and the Hampton Boat

Dick Pulsifer welcomes us with solid handshakes and apologizes that the shop is cold; he's been down to Portland getting ready for the Maine Boatbuilders Show. He fires up the stove, and the phone rings. He picks it up and talks while we admire the simplicity, detail, and craftsmanship of the strip-built boat-in-progress. Dick joins us, and I ask how he happened to get into the Hamptons he builds today.

"As a youngster, I summered on Yarmouth Island, off Cundy's Harbor. Boats like these were what fishermen were using in the late '40s. As small fry, we'd see them puttering around. We'd go out hauling with lobstermen, or go to the mainland with the caretaker to get the milk or whatever was needed. Many years later, when I came out of the navy, I found an old Hampton from the late '50s and bought her, with the idea of putting my one-lunger engine in it." Dick remembered well the look of the Hampton Boats of his youth, twisting and turning with ease as they worked their traps.

"When people ask about their shape," says Dick, "I tell them it's simpler to describe backwards. I ask, You know what Maine lobsterboats are? Well, this is the boat they evolved from. If it weren't any good, if it hadn't been comfortable to stand up in and work from, the shape would have atrophied, as many hull shapes have."

Starting in the early 1900s, Charlie Gomes became the master of the Hampton Boat and remained so for fifty or sixty years. The son of a Portuguese fisherman, Gomes was not an educated man, but he built more than two hundred boats, selling them all along the southwestern Maine coast. Dick Pulsifer's first boat, the *Kaly*, was a Gomes-built Hampton. She is now in the collection of the Maine Maritime Museum at Bath. "I felt good about pushing the museum to accept her," he says, "even though she was always used recreationally. It's the same boat as the ones that lobstered for years. The Hampton is a flexible design."

Dick enjoys telling how local fishermen would build their own boats, just as they did in Jonesport. "I've seen a lot of boats built with good cheer—not by professional boatbuilders but by a pickup crew, with the owner there. The boat might end up eight inches wider than the molds—the owner might have decided he'd like it a little different—but with strip planking, it doesn't matter, as long as the boat is the same on each side. It's not like carvel planking, where you've committed yourself on the first piece of wood."

Strip planking, which involves edge-fastening long, relatively narrow planking strips involves less of the careful sizing, shaping, and beveling that are required by the wider planks used in the carvel system. It also made use of cheaper lumber. "In Casco Bay," Dick says, "Hamptons and strip planking have always gone hand in hand. It's sensible—pine was abundant in this area and still is. At the sawmills, you see all those pieces left over—beautiful clear sapwood—that just lend themselves to becoming strips. In strip planking, all you need is nails, pine, and a sense of the shape you want. It's easy to master; like brickwork, it's a skill, but you can quickly learn the repetitive aspects of it."

Dick builds with strips that are nearly square in cross section: one and one-quarter inches by one and one-sixteenth inches. The older boats' strips, he says, were more rectangular. "Working with air-dried wood is harder than planking with the greener wood they would have used in earlier days. It doesn't like to twist. I've developed some techniques where the strips are stepped rather than twisted, so they're less apt to break."

Dick sees himself as following Charlie Gomes's legacy, and for the first fourteen or fifteen boats, he tried to be faithful to the originals. "But for the uses I'm putting them to," he says, "you don't need a wide washboard. Six inches will do instead of eight—you get more room inside, and you can still sit on the rail. And, it doesn't take a great leap of faith to see that the boat has much more appeal with remote controls, a diesel engine, and turn-key starting. But the essence of the Hamptons is represented right here," he says, indicating the hull before us.

"It's refined—it would be foolish to do them and not make them a little better—but I stay mindful of what makes them good. I get evangelical about these boats. The Hampton Gospel is: Keep it simple, keep it efficient. It's a sweet hull above and below the water. You just need people thinking not how fast they can go but how much they can enjoy being on the water. If you have to go eighteen knots, you ought to go elsewhere.

"Nearly all of these boats have gone into family service," Dick says. "Three are working in boatyards—and their owners play with them a lot, too.

If there's just a little sense and wisdom on the part of the helmsman—or woman—the Hampton'll bring you home. You can cruise the Erie Canal or the coast of Maine; you can take the proverbial cocktail cruise; or you can hang out and putter around different places. There's no place hairier than the mouth of the Kennebec River on the wrong tide, but you let these boats have their head—so the bow's up just a little, with the load distributed just right—and *bam!* you go right through."

The Pulsifer Hamptons are built-down boats, twenty-two feet long with a beam of six feet, eight inches. "As I've developed the hull, I've gained confidence in what my eye would like to see. I've widened the hull in the stern—not amidships—and with boat No. 48 I deepened the number three mold so it has more belly, so it's a little stiffer. You don't see it, but I can feel it. There's a little tuck in back—the bottom is just a little concave from the transom forward. You can't have too little stern, or the hull will squat, but if it's too broad then there'll be too little buoyancy forward. It comes back to balance. You can't add on balance—with trim tabs and so forth—in a boat that ought to know better.

"Working with just twenty-seven horsepower, things the big boys talk about just aren't important. In a boat that goes fast, you have to have flare and reserve buoyancy, but here, the rubber's on the road.

"On my watch, instead of trying to make the Hampton Boats exactly as they were, I'm making them finer in the beginning. Not fancy, but finished better."

A friend of Dick's says, "These boats know what to do with the water."

"Watch out, there's six or seven kayaks out there."
"Gives me somethin' to aim at."
"I hear those deep-sea kayaks, you gotta hit 'em twice to sink 'em."
"I got reverse, I can back over 'em."

—VHF radio conversation

Fishing Today
THE *JESSE F. CROSS*

R ed Robarts is one of only a few lobstermen to fish out of Camden any more; the harbor has been taken over by yachts. His boat—the *Jesse F. Cross*—is a bright green, fiberglass Stanley 36 from Mount Desert Island. "Jesse Cross was my grandfather, my mother's father," says Red. "A friend and I finished the boat off. He was the master builder, and I did all the labor—whatever I could do. I was trying to think of a name for her, and there were too many women in my family, so I just thought I'd name the boat after my grandfather."

The *Jesse F. Cross* is unusual among Maine lobsterboats in that the windows in her house slant *inward* from top to bottom, like those on many big ships. "The friend who did most of the building was an English guy," explains Red, "and they do it that way a lot over there. He told me I might like it, so I said, 'What the heck?'—it didn't cost any more. One of the benefits is all that room up underneath the canopy top for your electronic equipment; you're not banging your head into it all the time. My friend said it would keep the glare down, and it does, a little bit. I guess it's better in the spray, too. As far as I know, it was the first boat like that around—not that it's any big deal."

Red wouldn't do much different with the *Jesse F. Cross:* "She's not an extra fast boat—she has a small diesel, a GM 4-71—but it costs only $12 a day in fuel and oil to run her. The engine had been rebuilt when I got it, and it's been rebuilt a couple of times since—it's thirty years old or so. But it's real simple.

There's nothing fancy on the boat. I might get a radar this year—not because I don't know where I am, but I don't want to run over one of those schooners. And once in a while, there's a tugboat coming up the bay, and you can't always see him. More important, he can't see you—fiberglass doesn't show up real good on radar. I wouldn't want to get run over by one of them.

"My boat's a nice seaworthy boat, but it won't float if it's full of water. I guess that's the only thing I've got against that boat: it's got no flotation; if it fills up, it sinks."

The inward-slanting windows at the front of the house are more common on European workboats.

The *Jesse F. Cross* did sink seven or eight years ago. "Right at the float," says Red. "My cousin was here from Long Island, eating dinner at the Waterfront restaurant. He looked out and saw it there, then after his dinner he looked again, and it was gone. He thought I'd come and taken her, but I didn't have any idea the boat was sunk until the next morning, when I came down and couldn't find her. I happened to have a little owl on my antenna to keep away the seagulls, and I looked over there, and here was this owl, about a foot off the channel.

"Well, I was real lucky on raising the boat. I was going to get Prock Marine to bring her up, but they were busy. It was going to take them a week or two, and I wanted to get her up right away and get the water out of the engine. So Mike Hutchings came down. He had a dragger, the *Jo Ann,* and he tied onto my bow and dragged the boat up onto Laite Beach there. One of those cheap plastic through-hulls had let go—I'll never do that again.

"The insurance company came and looked at it, and they said they'd fix the engine. But it was October, and all my traps were set, and I had no way to get them. So the harbormaster at that time, Ken Miller, let me use his boat. It was smaller than mine, a little narrower, with a gas engine, and I just wasn't used to that boat." Red says he was accustomed to going across the bay and staying all day, expecting to scoot home after the wind had come up. "My boat would just punch through," he says, but he kept breaking windows in the borrowed boat.

"The only thing I liked about that wooden boat and that gasoline engine was the quietness. On my boat, you can't hear yourself think. I do wear those ear things, and it's soundproofed as much as possible, but still, there's a lot of noise in there.

Although Red is very much the seasoned lobster fisherman today, he wasn't born to it like so many others we met. He majored in geology and psychology in college. "I didn't have the slightest desire to go lobstering; that was the last thing I wanted to do," he says. He was going to work in social services, but he ended up going down to the West Indies as crew on a big catamaran. "A week or two after we left, I talked with my mother, and she said I'd gotten a call from the state saying I had a job. I just told her to tell them to give it to somebody else."

Red worked winters in the West Indies for a couple of years, coming home to Maine in June, when it started getting hot down there. Then one year, he heard from a Long Island friend who had a lobsterboat; the friend's wife had made him an ultimatum: either he or the boat had to go. "I didn't want a lobsterboat. What would I need one for?" asks Red. "But I got to thinking about it and decided it would be a pretty good life—to work on boats in the West Indies in the winter and to lobster in Maine during the summer. But the lobstering kind of got to me; I really enjoyed it. Then in '77, I decided to build a new boat. I made a few more yacht deliveries, but that was about it. I still have a lot of friends with sailboats, so I can go sailing most any time."

What is it about lobstering that got to him? Red laughs. "Well. I don't really know. Certainly the independence—but you could do a lot of things and be self-employed. When I was a kid, I certainly never thought I'd do it—no one in my immediate family fished. And twenty years ago was a real down time in lobstering—it was a good day if I could go out and get seventy-five pounds. I've learned a lot since, and there are a lot more lobsters." Red attributes this as much as anything to the government's cleaning up the water—stopping the factories from dumping their wastes directly into the rivers and bays.

"I sometimes worked at the tannery in Camden when I was in high school, and they had a pipe coming right out of the building. It was three or four feet in diameter, and when they opened up those vats, the stuff dumped right into the harbor. It used to stink, and there were little bits of leather and wool in the water. The sewerage went in there, too—of course, the lobsters liked that. And the wood chips from the sawmills covered the bay out here.

First it settled onto the spawning bottom, and then it depleted the oxygen when it started to degrade. So between the chemicals and the wood chips, that was the end of the fish out here.

"Ten or fifteen years ago—whenever it was they put a stop to that—I immediately saw a difference. That very same winter, a big salmon moved into the harbor here. It was a huge fish—three or four feet long. I saw quite a few Atlantic salmon out on the bay. Now, stripers are coming back, and the bottom's cleaning up. Course, the worms will eat the chips up in six months, if you don't keep adding to them. You leave a wooden trap out there six months, it's gone. Well, you might still have the shape, but that's all.

"We really manage the stock, here," he says. "I don't know of a lobsterman in Maine who would scrape the eggs off a female." In fact, doing so is illegal, but the mere logic of protecting spawning lobsters is enough to convince Maine lobstermen to mark the tails of berried females with a V-notch and release them. Still, Red—like others—says that not all fishermen refrain from scrubbing and selling "eggers."

"Those that do are draggers who catch lobsters accidentally—they bring up three or four hundred pounds of lobsters in the net, and they're worth three or four bucks a pound. They're not going to throw them overboard. Around here, though, there's no groundfish, so there's no draggers. But every year there's more guys fishing, and more traps, and more lobsters caught—it doesn't make any sense to the scientists. I heard one of them at one of those meetings. He admitted that he'd spent $250,000 on a study, but he said he learned more in a weekend of talking to lobstermen than he'd learned in all his studying."

Red fishes the area between Lincolnville and Rockport, and he goes across the bay to Mark and Lasell Islands and Robinson Rock. "It's an interesting place over there—there's always seals on the rocks, and there's an eagle that lives on Mark Island. He's so used to me now that he landed on my boat one time. I've never heard of an eagle landing on anyone's boat before. It was really foggy, and I knew I was up close to the island, the way the water was. I slowed down, and he just came out of the fog and landed right up on the bow of the boat, with his wings out. He was there for a couple of minutes, and then off he went."

Red has always fished alone. "I have a lot of seagulls, but no sternman. I'm thinking about getting someone to help me this year. My back bothers me a little bit, and if I fell overboard, then he could at least throw me a life jacket and call the Coast Guard and tell them where to find me." Red has 500 traps but only plans to fish 400. "We lose quite a few to boat traffic out here. On a few, the line gets worn through, or they get wrapped around something, but boat traffic accounts for most of them. It's nice to have a few extra on hand," he says.

"The *Appledore* [a passenger-carrying sailing vessel] got hundreds last year, literally hundreds, as near as we could figure. Seven of them all at once, one time. And there were a couple of fast commuters from Islesboro. I don't know if they're still coming across now, but they took a straight line no matter what, and they were cutting off traps left and right. They could have gone around. So I got a bunch of wooden buoys and tied them on instead of the foam ones. It wasn't but a couple of days before I went out and found one of those buoys, cut right in half. I bet they knew it when they hit that!

Red Robarts at the helm of the Jesse F. Cross.

"We realize we're taking our chances when we put out a trap. We do try to stay out of the channel, but you've got to go where the lobsters are. If the lobsters are in the channel, we've got to go there too. But I put my oldest traps out there."

Red's collected some interesting stories over the years. "About eight years ago, on one of those gray days with the wind coming across southeasterly, I was headed for some traps over by Lime Island. I got halfway across the bay and saw something that looked like a rowboat upside down. I thought uh-oh, and then I saw something flashing. As I got closer, I could see it was one of those

99

two-person kayaks, and there was someone in front all hunched up, and a guy in back paddling like mad. I asked, 'What's the problem?' and he said, 'My wife's having a baby.'"

Red chuckles. "Well, that was a first. The guy asked me, 'Could you tow us into Camden?' and I thought, That's a good idea—diesel exhaust fumes in their faces, and there she was thrashing around in the bow of this thing. So I said, 'You get on the boat, and we'll tie the kayak alongside.'

"They had put their boat in at the launching ramp at Camden and gone across to Saddle Island for the weekend. They spent one night, and the second night her water broke around two in the morning. Instead of going to North Haven, right behind them, they headed for Camden, which was twice as far. The guy was all wore out. He never would have gotten much farther; I think they both would have drowned.

"I got them on the boat and took them into Camden, and we got her off to the hospital just about in the nick of time. They decided to call the baby Jesse, after my boat. Afterward, I heard that she told someone I didn't say much to them, but what could I say? I couldn't believe that they were so stupid. I'd have been pretty rude if I'd said anything.

"Then there was one time with the old boat. It was a really hot, calm summer day in August, and I was out by the bell when I saw something flopping around in the water. It was a blue jay. I thought, Jeez, what happened to him? and I grabbed him. He didn't seem to be hurt; he was just really wet. So I wrapped him up in a towel and put him on the engine, and then I forgot all about him. I came in four or five hours later and unloaded the lobsters, while all the tourists were standing around and asking questions about why is the water so high or so low and wanting to see the lobsters. Then I remembered that blue jay, and I thought, He must be cooked on that hot engine all day. So I went down and kind of turned my back on everyone, not wanting them to see me unloading a dead bird. I opened up that towel . . . and he just flew away. 'What was that?' they wanted to know, and I just said, 'Oh, that's a blue jay. We always carry one around for good luck.'"

Red says he can tell the tourists most anything, and they'll believe him. "Mostly, they want to know how you can tell when the trap's full of lobsters." One day, Red's mother overheard two women talking. "One of them told the other that you can tell the trap is full because the little buoy goes under," he scoffs. "And they're always asking questions about the tide," says Red. "This one fellow was saying, 'Last night when I was here, this place was full of water, so how come now you can see all that grass and all the rocks and the mooring chains and all that?' I said, 'Well, it's low tide.' And he asked, 'Can't they do it at night when nobody'll see it?'"

Several of Red's tales involve not tourists but close calls he has survived: "One winter, I hauled my boat out, but I had a few lobsters in a crate over here in the middle of the harbor, tied to a float. A friend wanted a few for Christmas, so I'd saved him some. A couple of days before Christmas, I rowed out in my skiff. Well, the float had about a foot of ice and snow on it, and it was late in the afternoon, it was dark, and there wasn't a soul around. I pulled my skiff up on the float. When I got the crate up, I slipped, and my foot went out, hit the skiff, and knocked it right off the float. I was barehanded, and all I had on was a vest. I looked around, and I thought, This is nice! But the skiff had gone off upwind, and I thought, Well, that skiff's going to come by pretty soon. It did, but it was coming about twenty feet away."

Red knew he didn't have much chance of jumping for it, and he certainly didn't want to spend the night out there. "So I dug around in the snow on the float, and there was a little bit of rope—pot warp. I grabbed a lobster and put a half hitch around him. When the boat came by, I swung him out, and he caught under the seat, and I hauled the skiff back in."

That wasn't the only time Red found himself in serious trouble. "When I had my old boat, I ran over something coming across the bay. It got caught in my propeller. I thought it was a piece of rope, and I went over the side to look. It was this chain with a rope and a wooden thing on it. That was August, about the hottest day of the year, but the water was still pretty cold. I was down there prying this thing apart, and I pried it right around my wrist. I got a little concerned then. I got my arm out, eventually, but it was torn up good, and I was hanging on the side of the boat. The water was so cold, I guess I had hypothermia.

"A fisherman from Rockport came by—Howard Kimball, he's not alive anymore—and said, 'What are you doing, taking a bath?' Anyhow, he got me on the boat, and he towed me in. I don't go over the side any more. I call somebody to come get me."

"Susan Jean, *you there?*"

"*Yup.*"

"*How's the old man, still alive?*"

"*He's still kickin'.*"

"*Still tip his neck back?*"

"*Yup, and bend his elbow, too*"

—VHF radio conversation

The Gentleman Tow-boater
JIM SHARP AND THE *MAINE*

In the mid-1970s, the people at the Department of Marine Resources decided they wanted three patrol boats, and they wanted all three to be built in Maine. They were much taken with a half-model carved by Lyford Stanley of Bass Harbor, and the project was set into motion.

John Letcher of AeroHydro in Southwest Harbor did the lofting on his computer instead of the floor. He then carried the data on the back of his bicycle to a different computer in Orono, where the patterns were printed on huge pieces of paper. Finally, John and boatbuilder Jock Williams transferred the boat's lines to plywood using pinpricks. (This was the first full-scale lofting done on a computer. Since then, AeroHydro has developed what is arguably the most comprehensive marine-design software on the market. It has been used in such projects as the *America's* Cup boats, including the New Zealand boat that won in '95.)

In 1977, Jock launched the *Maine*—the first forty-four-footer from Stanley's design. He built her as a "one-off," using panels of Airex foam sheathed inside and out with fiberglass, then made a mold from her to build others. Although the Marine Patrol was happy with the boat—finding it a very stable and rugged vessel—they only took delivery of one more Stanley 44. Jock, however, has sold fifty-seven so far, all working boats. "It was designed to make easy transitions from fishery to fishery," says Jock. "It can lobster, do light dragging, gillnetting, even tuna. Neither the boat or its gear are so big you can't make the changes easily. It was kind of ahead of its time, really," he says. "With all the restrictions on fishermen now—limiting what they can do in one fishery—a man can switch around and make a living with that boat."

Though he's not a fisherman, Jim Sharp of Camden wanted just that sort of versatility: "I was looking for a boat to do some towing and this and that," he says, "and I wanted it fiberglass because I was tired of working on wooden vessels." (Not too long before, Jim had retired his windjammer, the 121-foot Gloucester fishing schooner *Adventure*.) A friend of his suggested the *Maine*, a former Marine Patrol boat. "He told me there was nothing wrong with her. She had a beautiful engine—they'd blown its predecessor and had to replace the block. Then they laid her up, so her engine was essentially brand new. A couple of months earlier, they had put her up for auction, but they didn't advertise the event properly, and no one came.

"That was the year they couldn't keep the statehouse doors open because they were desperate for money. So, I made them a ridiculous offer. Well, they said they couldn't accept it. But she had a sixty-four-mile radar on her, and I certainly didn't want it, so I told them I'd leave the radar and meet them partway on the price. They said all right.

"For the Marine Patrol," says Jim, "the *Maine* had chased the lobstermen around, making sure they weren't taking short lobsters, and they all knew her. So, when I first got her, every time I saw a lobster fisherman, he was going the other way. I felt like I had the plague."

Jim bought the *Maine* as a water taxi and for towing and other commercial uses. "I just don't get a kick out of getting in the boat and going across the bay for no reason—I've done it for so many years with a purpose," he says. There is a WATER TAXI sign in the *Maine's* window, and Jim gets referrals from the local chamber of commerce and the Camden harbormaster. "Most of it is taking people out on sightseeing trips, people who don't want to go in the party boats—the *Betselma* and *Lively Lady* and so on. They want to see the seals, ospreys—and whales, of course," he chuckles. There aren't many whales in Penobscot Bay.

He says that lighthouses are always high on the priority list, and sometimes he takes his passengers to Stonington or Vinalhaven to see a real fishing village. "I point out homes of the rich and famous," says Jim, "but mostly they're more interested in the beauty of the islands and the sea life. I get two or three jobs a week that way. And I'm always listening to the radio to see if there's a boat in distress—that happens two or three times a season. But I'm a gentleman towboater," Jim says. "I make six to ten deliveries a year. One year, a building crew was doing renovations out on one of the islands. It was a foggy summer, so the airplanes couldn't fly. I had a pretty fast boat, so I took them just as quick."

He tells of transporting the Quasimodal Chorus out to Swans Island for the annual folk-sing out there: "We all sang our way over, and coming back we took the offshore route—around Isle au Haut and Vinalhaven—and we ran into a school of whales. The chorus sang to the whales, hoping the whales were singing back to them.

"Then there was the time when a woman on the day-boat *Betselma* suffered a reaction to a bee sting and was in shock. Well, I had a fast boat, so I took the medication and ran it out to the *Betselma*. I stuck my hand out my pilothouse window, and Les Bex stuck his hand out of *Betselma*'s window. I was going through his wake and he was going through mine. We'd each slowed down, but we went past each other at about six knots. I slapped the medication right in his hand, and he administered it. The woman was fine by the time they got in.

Originally built for the Department of Marine Resources, the Maine *now handles a variety of tasks.*

"Course, I've done towing jobs—boats off ledges, broken-down boats out on the bay, boats from Camden to Rockland or elsewhere—it's all in a day's work. Once there was an eighty-foot motoryacht on the ledges off Camden. They saw the red buoy on one side and the green buoy on the other, so they went between them and fetched her right up hard. There were decks and decks on this boat, and a uniformed crew. As the tide came up, we carefully slid her off—she was taking on quite a lot of water—and we pulled her into Wayfarer.

"Then there was the lighthouse tour: A woman was making a book of photographs of lighthouses, so we went around looking at all of the lighthouses on this part of the coast. That was a great charter."

Jim gets quieter. "When Erland 'Cappy' Quinn died—he'd worked for me for fifteen years—I took the burial casket and the funeral party out to Eagle Island, where Cappy grew up. That was the nicest funeral ever. We went up on the hill there—you can see all over the bay—and it was a gorgeous day. The cemetery plot had been dug by hand; they don't have any machinery out there." A service was said by the minister from the *Sunbeam*, which serves as a Christian mission to the islands. "God's tugboat," Jim calls her. "Everybody sang *Amazing Grace*—it was so moving. And the grave was filled in by hand. It was a real old-time down east funeral, the kind Cappy would have liked.

"I've done both a marriage and a burial aboard the *Maine*—at different times, of course," Jim says. "One man had lived in Rockport all his life, but he moved away to be with his family in his waning years. When he died, we carried his ashes out—appropriately—to the deep water off the Graves," he says, referring to a ledge off Rockport.

"Spencer Schuyler was a classical pianist I had known from the schooner. He had come on the *Adventure* as a passenger, and that's when I found out he was a pianist. For three or four years after that, I got him to come with a cellist and a violinist, and we had classical music all week. I had a piano aboard, a sixty-six-key Melody Grand; it was the size of a harpsichord, you know—perfect for chamber music. We found it in a hock shop someplace. We tuned it every year when Spencer came.

"When he wanted to get married, he asked me if I'd do the ceremony. The *Adventure* was in Gloucester then, so we took the *Maine* out to Lasell Island. It was one of those beautiful days, with a slight ripple on the water and the Camden hills in the background. It was a perfect ceremony. We had champagne and cake and the whole works, then a gang of us went ashore on Lasell and spent the rest of the day there, roaming the beach.

"Eventually they were divorced, though," Jim says, "so that tells you what kind of a splice I made."

Jim is happy with the *Maine*. "She's seaworthy as the devil—you could take her to Labrador and feel just fine. And she's so handy, you could pound nails in the wharf with her." At the time I spoke with him, Jim said he had pleasure plans for her—to take her in stages to New York, up the Hudson, out the Erie and Oswego Canals to Lake Ontario, through the Trent-Severn Canal, through Georgian Bay to Lake Huron, then to Mackinac and Lake Michigan, down to Chicago, down the Mississippi to Cairo, out the Tennessee River to the Tombigbee, and across the Gulf of Mexico to Florida, where the gentleman tow-boater winters.

Says Jim, "You have to have dreams, don't you?"

PETER KASS
Smoothness in Wood

We meet Peter at Moody's Diner one day in May, after his shop has closed for the evening. He's a tall man—in his forties, I'd guess—with an easy smile and no pretension.

"I built my first lobsterboat in '86," he explains. "I had the shop four or five years before that, building small pleasure boats and doing a lot of railway stuff—like hauling lobsterboats in June. Back then there was still a good dragger business, and they'd haul out summer and fall. It was pretty much just me, but I had steady work.

"I didn't set out to build lobsterboats—it's a niche I just sort of fell into. It takes 2,500 man-hours, about five months, to build one. I have two guys working for me, on average. We just have one boat going at a time. It's really skilled labor that makes us tick—I have a good crew now, and I wouldn't know where to go to replace any of them. If you started with an average crew, it would probably take double the hours, and you couldn't afford it.

Peter has to compete with the fiberglass-boat builders, and that means he needs experienced, motivated employees. "At the price we sell our boats for, there's no margin to support a guy that isn't producing," he explains. Yet, finding the right people isn't easy. "I wish there were more [wooden-boat builders] out there—but there aren't. With just Ralph Stanley and me, there's nowhere people can get the experience. And the average guy would make more money building houses, unless he wanted to take the time to develop the skill and get paid well. You get a lot of dreamy sorts drift in, but what they do isn't worth what you pay them. It seems that the more people you have, the less they do."

Peter says that a wooden boat doesn't really cost any more than a good fiberglass boat, noting, "The machinery is a good part of the expense, and that's equal either way." He explains that the high overhead that characterizes Maine's large builders—buildings, tools, employees, insurance, heat, and the like—hikes the price of their boats and makes his own more competitive. He says, however, "There are a lot of little outfits, and we probably can't compete with them. But to finish 'glass well costs a lot—coring the hull laminate, endless sanding and finishing, and everything. I have done some 'glass jobs in the past, but we now avoid them." Peter says that he has nothing against fiberglass—he just doesn't want to build hulls with it.

"But part of what's made us successful," he notes, "is that we're not afraid to use 'glass where it makes sense, to make a wooden boat low in maintenance. Plywood and fiberglass decks, for instance—they're better. And PVC [solid plastic] rails. Those used to be oak, which didn't hold paint; with PVC, the maintenance on our boats is way down. And we usually put 'glass sheathing where they haul the traps up. We've got a new gimmick with stainless-steel flat bars and built-up fiberglass; we rout the edges into the hull so it's all flush, with no catches. It's pretty indestructible. And we've worked out a system with the scuppers [deck drains], where we have 'glass sealing the sides and a thick flange routed into the hull, so there's a 'glass tunnel right through. It's cheap. A bronze scupper will set you back $100; this is a lot less.

"One of the plusses to wood is that it absorbs vibration. The more wood you have, the better off you are. When you're running along in a 'glass boat, it may feel pretty smooth, but if you look around, everything is shaking. Our boats just hum. There's none of that crap going on. Of course Glenn Holland will disagree," he chuckles, acknowledging the glass builders' belief in their own product.

"There is more maintenance to a wooden boat, no question. If they weren't more comfortable, people wouldn't buy them. Five years ago, we built one for Bob Williams from Stonington. He says, 'You have two weeks of misery for fifty weeks of pleasure.' This guy is fifty-five years old and works hard. Down my way, the hardest-going fishermen don't put on two thousand hours a year, but this guy does twenty-five hundred. His knees were bothering him a lot with his glass boat—he was really in pain and wondered how long he could keep it up. But he's a lot better with a wood boat." And Williams isn't the only such case. "I built a boat for another guy who started with a wood boat and then had three glass boats before he got mine," says Peter. "He tells me, 'Now I can stay out longer on rougher days, and when I finally get home, I've still got some life left.'

"I just finished one for Bob Williams's son, John," Peter continues. "His old boat was a Newman 46, very heavily finished off, and he burned a lot of fuel. The new one—with just as many traps, working a little faster and just as comfortably—uses a fifth the fuel. John told me, 'If I never sell it, the fuel saving will make the payments on the old boat.'"

Like most boatbuilders, regardless of the material they work in, Peter Kass has found that different fishermen have different ideas about how a boat should be set up. "We used to have a dashboard that was two feet from front to back," he recalls, "but one fellow said, 'You're putting the windshield too far ahead; I want it close enough that I can cram my head out the window when it comes in foggy.' So we shortened up the dash. But then John Williams said he wanted more room. He wasn't going to have an opening window; he was going to have Clearviews," says Kass, referring to the rapidly spinning, circular windshield wipers often installed on bigger vessels.

Designed by Carroll Lowell, Kass's boats are finer forward with more flare than the average hull.

"Like a lot of Stonington boats, John's old one was left-handed [with the wheel and controls to port], but the new one we built him is right-handed. 'If you get a new boat every ten years,' he says, 'and if you change sides every time, then you'll wear evenly.' His father always had a left-handed boat, though, and says he'd never be able to run a right-handed one.

"A lot of young guys wouldn't think of a wooden boat," Peter laments, "but they don't know what they're missing. If an old guy comes down to see me and I'm working on a boat, it's ten minutes before he comes up the ladder to talk; he's looking around underneath, to see how it's put together. And then when he comes up, he's still looking around. But young guys come right up the ladder, asking how long the platform is, stuff like that. They don't know what they're looking at.

"Right now," says Peter, "the lobster business is such that people aren't really asking so much about the price of the boat; they're feeling pretty comfortable. It's not unheard-of for a guy to bring in a hundred thousand pounds a year, while ten years ago, thirty thousand was a lot, and a super-killer guy might get fifty thousand. But so far this spring, there's no lobsters in a lot of places. In my area, they're getting a pound a trap, but in Stonington, it's really dismal. Last year at this time, they got two pounds a trap, but this year—nothing. Spring fishing's always like that: some years it pays, some years it doesn't.

Kass works atop the framing for one of his wooden lobsterboats

"In '89, lobster prices fell through the floor, and interest rates were up. Everyone was scared to death, selling lobsters for what they'd gotten ten years before. My phone never rang. One guy canceled. I went from a four-boat backup to a year without an inquiry. In '90, I built Bob Williams's boat, then there weren't any more to build. We had just enough repairs to keep Rene and me going—we kept saying 'This is it, the end,' but then something else would come along. Finally, an order came in. Now I'm booked up four years ahead. A fellow came from Swans Island for the launching of John Williams's boat, and as soon as he saw her, he ordered one. When they got her home, a fellow from Matinicus saw her and ordered one.

"Ralph Stanley's got this niche with Friendship sloops—he couldn't begin to compete in price with a Sabre [a Maine-built production fiberglass sailboat] or something like it, but his customers wouldn't even consider one of those." Peter explains that his situation is different: "People who come to me aren't going to pay an extra $50,000 for a wooden boat. There are buyers out there who say 'I want what I want and the price be damned,' but I haven't hooked up with one of them.

"Boatbuilding used to be a seven-days-a-week thing for me," Peter says, "I don't do that so much any more. But if we've got a keel all ready for a coat of red lead on Friday, I'll go down Saturday so on Monday, it'll be ready. Sometimes if you don't stay the extra hour, you lose a whole day the next day. I'm lucky; my crew is flexible. If it takes two hours to paint a hull, and we only have an hour left, I can ask, 'You want to quit an hour early, or stay an hour late?' A big outfit can't do that. The bell rings, and they're all gone.

"Most of my boats have been forty-footers—Carroll Lowell's design," Peter explains. "The smallest working boat I've built is thirty-six feet, a twenty-year-old Carroll Lowell model. But fishermen are putting the same machinery in a 36 as they do in a 40. I figured it up for a guy, and to go to a 40 the way he wanted it rigged would have cost just 5 percent more than a 36. So, you might as well go for the bigger boat."

Peter Kass obviously has a great appreciation for the design talent of his chief collaborator, the late Carroll Lowell. "His boats are fantastic," says Peter, "particularly the built-down ones. We've done both built-down and skeg, and up to thirty-six feet, you might as well go skeg. But in recent years, everyone's deepened the boat to swing a bigger wheel. If you need thirty inches of clearance, you need a built-down boat.

"Carroll's designs are comfortable, and they don't pound. Compared to other boats, his are finer and deeper forward, and they have more flare. There's a hollowness to the whole forward part—above and below the waterline. They're very pretty and comfortable, and they go extremely well. They go *through* the water, instead of over it, like the Jonesporters or the Hollands. Our boat's in the water all the time but going right along. With a 300-horsepower Caterpillar, they'll go over twenty knots. They pick up some but run much more level than most. You can see over the bow all the time—there's none of that seeing nothing but trunk cabin as they pick up their bows.

"And, they have enough flare that in an extreme situation, it's hard to put the bow underwater. One guy told me he couldn't put the bow under, but that was before he went to Cashes Ledge. After he went out there, I asked him, 'You put the bow under yet?'

" 'Oh, God,' he said, 'I put the whole boat under, but it doesn't hurt her a bit.'

"I'm quite a spy," admits Peter. "Every chance I get to look at anyone else's boat, I do, and I pick up stuff. Carroll had a lot of influence on me, but I've come up with things on my own, too. The boat I'm doing now is my design. She's a little fuller forward, because the guy's going to put a heavy engine in her. And she's a little shoaler. Carroll kept getting deeper, which is good from a performance standpoint, but it gets in the way of turning a little bit. And you don't get the lift.

"Our boats are just good looking. Right now, we've pretty much got all the angles right. And you can't do that with a molded fiberglass house, because there, you have to keep a minimum radius to everything; you can't get the sharp angles, the clean look. We finish off each boat like a yacht—it doesn't cost that much more, and it's easier to clean as well as looking better.

"I like the looks of lobsterboats, and I just like that they go out and do what they're supposed to do every day. Building yachts is neat, and it's nice to admire them, but they can't compare to something that's working, day in and day out, doing something productive, making two guys a living. And on the whole I've found fishermen to be fantastic customers. Never built a boat for a guy that hasn't been just great. A lot of them just stop by to visit. One guy from Plymouth, Massachusetts, hasn't missed a launching.

"I work awful hard, and I make a living," says Peter. "But if I put in just 2,000 hours a year, like the average American, I'd starve. I worked eleven hours today, happy as hell every minute. I wouldn't trade it for four hours of 'glass work for the same money. I throw in things I don't get paid for—if the specs call for four coats of paint, but it's a little rough and doesn't look just right, I'll sand it down and give it another coat and not charge. Chances are no one'll even know, but it makes it fun.

"I really do love this work."

"That's Seal Island, and if it don't get the hell out of the way, we're goin' to run right over it."

—Robin Quimby, Islesboro

QUICKSILVER
An Island Lifeline

It's eleven o'clock Saturday morning, February seventeenth. This is Earl on a recording. Bonnie and I are out for a bit, but if you'd like to leave a message, go ahead after the beep. The ferry is being worked on, so we'll be making a few runs back and forth. We expect to be in Lincolnville around noon. We'll be bringing the parts back for the ferry, so you can check with the Lincolnville terminal for the exact time. We expect the ferry will be running again later this afternoon, but if not, we'll make a late afternoon trip to bring folks back. We'll update this machine when we know better, or you can try us on the boat. The number is. . . ."

Earl MacKenzie runs a year-round island taxi service from Islesboro in *Quicksilver*, a Calvin Beal–designed South Shore 34 built to Earl's own rugged specifications. "Our primary mission is serving the people of Islesboro," Earl says. "We're a backup to the ferry—part of the emergency system on Islesboro—and we provide after-hours transportation for the school's athletic, academic, and social events." He's taken high-schoolers in full dress to their inter-island proms for three years now. "We also accept outside contracts unrelated to Islesboro—from Tenants Harbor to Bar Harbor—to help defray the costs of owning the boat," says Earl. "But, we turn down any charters that would keep us from being available on the island at night."

To Earl, *Quicksilver* epitomizes the evolution of the Maine lobsterboat, the transition from the days of the early built-down hulls to the time when it occurred to someone that to build the boat on a skeg would be faster. *Quicksilver* represents a further refinement: she has a hollow skeg which, when filled with water, provides even more stability than the keel of a built-down boat. "I don't know where the pinnacle will be," Earl says. "We may be pretty close to it. If the hulls get much wider, they'll spank.

"The Maine lobsterboat is one of the most seakindly, able boats in the world. They're fast, and they're distinctive because they get their speed with a relatively small amount of power. A lot of yachts take twice the horsepower to do what a lobsterboat does. And they're fairly reasonable in cost by comparison to yachts—though you can put a lot into one, of course."

The water taxi Quicksilver *moves people and cargo to and from Islesboro regardless of the weather.*

Quicksilver is cored in construction, which is to say that end-grain balsa sheets were sandwiched between the layers of fiberglass fabric in her hull laminate. Earl explains, however, that there's no core directly under the engine, and the lack of insulation from the cool seawater moderates the temperature of the engine compartment. He thinks that the boat's cored construction, heavier laminate, and reinforcing timbers make *Quicksilver* more rigid than many 'glass boats and gives her a feel more like that of a wooden boat.

"She has proven real seaworthy," Earl says. "We've had her out in some pretty awful conditions." The Islesboro ferry quits when conditions are too bad, but the need for people to get ashore doesn't stop. Earl has made runs for medical emergencies ranging from sick dogs to midwives en route to island birthings. These situations don't wait. "We go out in ridiculous weather, really," he says, "but she holds up."

Sometimes the treacherous trips are for pleasure—someone's pleasure, not Earl's. Fall duck-hunting expeditions, for example, are notorious. He remembers one particular group he took out in late November: "We were almost to North Haven, and it was quite rough—eight-foot seas, once in a while over ten. It was debatable whether we should have been out there, but we thought we'd find somewhere to drop those guys. This one hunter from Kentucky was a little bit cocky, kind of blabbing away. He was probably nervous and trying to sound brave, but he sort of got to me.

"We keep our life jackets under the seats, and I looked at him and said quietly, but just loud enough that he could hear, 'Would you mind passing me a life jacket?' He started to do it and then stopped, and the color drained from his face. I thought he was going to throw up, but he didn't. Everyone stopped talking, and then I smiled and said I was just kidding. But he didn't say too much after that. Pretty soon they decided maybe it was too rough, and asked if we could turn back."

I ask Earl about problems he's had with ice. "Normally, it takes ten minutes to run over to Lincolnville," he says. "But sometimes, it's taken as much as two hours. One night, I got stuck. There was four to six inches of ice, with slush on top. The *Quicksilver* has heat exchangers instead of keel pipes for cooling the engine, and when the pump sucks up that saltwater slush and it fills up the sea strainer, there's no circulation and the engine overheats. You have to stop and clean out the heat exchanger, then start up again.

"There was one week I didn't run at all. She was frozen in at the dock. Then Thursday a week ago, I went across thinking it wouldn't be too bad, but there were chunks of freshwater ice over two feet thick that had come down the river. Once in a while, a bunch of those would get together, and I'd stop and try to gradually move them aside to get through. It didn't hurt the hull—though I wouldn't want to do too much more of it—but it bent the prop and took most of the paint off the bottom. At one point, I thought we were going to have to get off and walk. We made it, though, but we had to haul the boat to put a new prop on.

"Two years ago, the bay froze," recalls Earl. "The Lubec basketball teams were here, and I was going to take them across after the game. At half time, I scooted out to see what it was like. I hit ice and the boat slid up on top of it; then ice filled in behind me. It was hard to back off again. Finally I got her in and turned around. Those teams spent the night—I couldn't take them off."

Earl says he likes being out in the winter, as long as the boat is comfortable. *Quicksilver* cruises at sixteen or eighteen knots, and she is very heavily insulated, so she is quiet. Because the boat is certified by the Coast Guard to carry passengers and because of Earl's interest in search-and-rescue missions and winter trips, she has equipment and safety features a lot of boats don't have. *Quicksilver* carries a sophisticated radar, both GPS and loran position-finding systems, an automatic fog horn, a loud-hailer, a heated window and spinning Clearview wiper, and all kinds of lighting. She also has two heaters, which Earl says make more noise than the engine. Her house is all enclosed, although there is a sliding door by the steering station, so the helmsman can reach out to catch a line or give a hand to someone.

"When you run in the winter, you take more precautions," says Earl. "You take extra anchors, listen to the weather very carefully, and stay a little farther off a lee shore. Nothing is forgiving out there.

"Even the water seems harder."

"I don't care who the man is nor how smart he is, you run him long enough in the fog and sooner or later he'll hit something."

—Went Durkee, Islesboro

WENT DURKEE AND THE *OWL*

"**H**ow did Mr. Moseley come to buy the Owl?" I ask Islesboro's Went Durkee, who has been the caretaker for the Moseley family since 1964. I only knew why our family had sold the Newbert and Wallace lobster yacht—my parents were buying a sailboat.

"He asked me what I thought of her," remembers Went, "and I told him I thought she was about the best-built boat around. Later, I asked Willis Rossiter if I'd bragged her up too much, and he said I hadn't." Willis would have known; he was the best shipwright on the island.

"That boat's double timbered and double fastened," says Went. "She's the model they built to fish off Monhegan with, only they got an eighteen-foot open cockpit on 'em. They don't start lobsterin' out there till January. She's self-bailin'—you dump a half a ton of water in the cockpit, and in no time at all, it all goes away. She's just as solid as the day she was built. Had to do a lot of work on the side of the cabin—where you lower the windows, fresh water got in—but that's all fixed now. I've run the *Owl* since 1964, and the Moseleys haven't made a call for me yet when I haven't met them.

"I've given them some hellish rides," admits Went. "One time we was over in Castine, and it had come up to blow. They come down to the dock and said, 'Mrs. Moseley says we better stay over and go home in the morning.' I said, 'Well, you tell Mrs. Moseley that I'm headin' for home, and I'll be back for her in the morning.' Pretty soon they come back and told me, 'Mrs. Moseley says if you're going home, she's comin' home with you.' I'll admit the *Owl* rolled and threw some water around, but she come.

"She's some different than when you knew her," he tells me. "Now she has a 265-horsepower International V-8 in her—you get her into a hard place, and you can handle her. When they put that big motor in, Al Norton told me if I ran her at 3,000 rpm like I did the old one, she wouldn't use any more gas than she did with the other engine. But I run her at 2,500 anyway, and she goes along fine. No use trying to get a lot of speed from her—she wasn't built for it. She was built to be able. Everybody's in such a hell of a hurry." (One day, we were talking with a young Islesboro man who said, "You don't want to get behind Went on the road. There ain't no one slower.")

Last year, the *Owl* got new side curtains. As Went tells it, "Mrs. Moseley said, 'They've started leaking, I don't know why,' and I said, 'No reason they shouldn't, they've been on since 1957.' "

Went Durkee relaxes aboard the **Owl**, *which he has cared for since 1964.*

After Mr. Moseley, senior, died, the family sold the big house and the land on the point. Went now works for young Fred, himself a grandfather. "This year, Fred's going to be out there a week and be gone a week, and the gaps in between will be filled in with kids and dogs. Everybody's got a golden retriever," says Went. "The *Owl*'s just the boat they need. She's not any too big. When they come for a weekend, you can't imagine the amount of stuff they bring. They bring collapsible dog pens, lawnmowers that blow bubbles for the kids to play with—all sorts of stuff. She used to bring this big dish with some kind of tomato sauce in it, and when the boat would rock some, that stuff would slop out one side, and then out the other side. Well, she hasn't brought it lately, not since I said, 'For Christ's sake, ain't you ever heard of Ragu?' Damn dish."

Went says that, for the most part, the family members themselves keep to smaller boats. "They had this little Mako [an open, center-console outboard]," he recalls. "It was the wettest thing—didn't take the chop good at all. People get these Clorox bottles and then wonder why they ain't much in a sea. Well, they went over to Lincolnville and picked up some people for lunch one time, and it breezed up in the afternoon. They called me and said they thought maybe I should take them back to the mainland in the *Owl*.

"It was some rough. She buried her bow right up to the windshield three times, but she'd get up and shake herself off. The spray just kept comin' up over her. I was steerin', and they was all huddled up in the cabin with me—young couple and a baby. And when we got there, I didn't even have to tie up. When we got close enough to the float, they just got off—didn't say nothin' about wantin' to come back again, neither. When I got back, Fred said he knew right where we was the whole time; he couldn't see us, but he could see the spray comin' up all the way. 'I'd have gotten them wet in the Mako,' Fred said. 'You'd 'a' drowned them,' I told him."

Though Went may scorn some modern-day products that don't do their jobs, he has a lot of respect for equipment that works. "We just got a new radar for the *Owl*, and it works nice," he says. "It's a lot lighter—she don't roll so bad with all that stuff down off'n there. Old one weighed 300 pounds; the new one's just eighteen. It's something, that's certain. You can see everythin' in the bay and which way it's goin'. That radar's the greatest invention.

"One time we was comin' home from Castine in the fog, and Mr. Moseley kept givin' me courses. Then he realized he'd skipped a course. But we was right where we was supposed to be. 'How'd we get here? I missed a course!' he asks me." Went smiles a little. He'd just been watching the radar and heading home.

"I used to take the help from the cottage every Thursday, their day off. Well, the first stop was Camden and the liquor store, then they wanted to go fishin'. We ended up over by Vinalhaven one time, and the fog come in. One of those guys was down in the cabin looking at the chart, and he asked me what course I'd take to run home. I told him, 'I haven't the faintest idea.' 'How do you get home, then?' he asked me. I said, 'Christ, a man ought to know how to get home.'"

"But you know, we've lived in the best time," says Edna, Went's wife.

"That's right," he responds. "It was hard, back then, but we got all this new stuff now, and I don't know as life is any better."

"My father was a smart man, a really good skipper. Back in those days, you didn't have radar and a fathometer and all that stuff—you sailed by the seat of your pants. I learned a lot from him. I didn't want to, but I did. I used to get seasick, and I said to myself, If I'm lucky enough to grow up, I'll never set foot on another boat.

"But I've spent my whole life on boats."

—Corliss Holland

FAST LOBSTERBOATS
The Holland Family's Obsession

As Glenn Holland was finishing up his tour in the Coast Guard, he asked his father to buy him a twenty-two-foot lobsterboat hull to finish off. "No, I ain't buyin' you a twenty-two-footer," Corliss told him. "But I'll buy you a thirty-footer."

Glenn started his boatbuilding business with that thirty-foot Repco. "I got the bare hull and finished it off on spec," he says. "It was sold before it was done, and I had an order for another, and two more were ordered before that one went out the door." In all, Glenn says, he and his father finished off fifteen or sixteen boats. "But people kept seeing those, and saying, 'Jeez, I wish somebody would build a bigger thirty-footer.' I heard it often enough that I thought, Well, I can do it."

Basing his design on the Jonesport–Beals boats he had always admired, but making it a little wider, a little deeper, with a little more flare in the bow, Glenn drew up the basic lines for a thirty-footer and made a half model. He took it to the late Royal Lowell, Will Frost's grandson and Carroll's older brother. "I want to build a boat that looks good, works good, and goes like hell," Glenn told Royal. "I suppose that'll be tough."

Glenn says Royal's face lit up like a Christmas tree. "No," said the designer, "I think we can do it." Between them, they finalized the boat's shape.

Beginning in 1976, the Hollands built twenty-five 30s and sent them to fishermen from Bar Harbor to New Jersey.

Then the mold burned. The hulls were being laid up in a shop in East Boothbay. "That place was an accident waiting to happen," says Glenn. "And when it did, my mold happened to be in it." Before replacing the tooling, he called around to people who'd bought his boats. "Everyone was pretty happy," he says, "but one guy said he might like it a couple of feet longer. Royal said the boat might go a little faster if it was longer. That did it." The new model measured thirty-two feet overall, and what is now accepted as a classic fiberglass lobsterboat was created. In November 1996, the crew at Holland's Boat Shop launched hull No. 111. About half the boats have been built to work, half for pleasure use.

The Holland 32 **Red Baron** *tears up the racecourse. Note how little of the hull remains in the water.*

As the business expanded, Royal Lowell's son Bill helped Glenn design a thirty-eight-foot model, and the first one was built in 1986. "The 38 has taken off," says Cathy, Glenn's wife. "The 32 was designed just as a workboat; no one cared about headroom. But the 38 is real roomy; it makes a nice yacht, too."

Glenn says, "Fishermen want boats bigger and bigger nowadays. But they don't have to be ugly. What's got into designers? They're drawing with a straight edge and a square. And I have no respect at all for boats that push half the ocean and drag the rest behind them."

Glenn speaks of one well-known racing lobsterboat: "Everybody was real impressed with her, but I never was. She went reasonably well, but you had to be in front of her in a race—if you was behind her, she'd drag all the water with her, and you'd go aground." In fact, there are a lot of designs he doesn't think much of. "The builder'll say, 'Well, our boats don't pound.' Of course they don't—they don't go fast enough!" insists Glenn.

Although he's a boatbuilder, Glenn says his interest is in design. But Cathy counters that the most important thing to him is speed. Glenn admits, "If it doesn't go fast, I'm not interested." As a small boy in Stonington, where his family had a house overlooking the thoroughfare, Glenn got up every morning to watch the lobsterboats. "I wore out the arm of that chair, sitting on it with my feet on the seat, looking out that window."

At first, Corliss Holland was lobstering on his own; later, he went to work on a lobster smack, delivering lobsters from Nova Scotia to Montauk Point. That boat was tied up at Billings Marine in Stonington when she was home. "I hung out there," Glenn says. "I was a regular shadow to my father—I don't know as I've given it up yet." So the younger Holland grew up around lobsterboats, and it was always the older Jonesport–Beals boats he liked best. They had the prettiest lines—and it turned out they were the fastest, too. ("Just coincidentally," Glenn says with a twinkle in his eye.)

"Most any harbor you went into, nine times out of ten, the fastest boat was from Beals. But I didn't really get interested in racing, then." Glenn adds, "Course, there's always racing—one guy comes around an island one way, and another comes the other way, and suddenly there they are, side by side. Then *pfft*, off they go!"

Glenn attributes the onset of what both he and his wife describe as their disease—lobsterboat racing—to an article in the commercial-fishing trade paper *National Fisherman* back in the '60s. "They were doing crazy things—not as crazy as we do now, but crazy for those days—Cadillac engines and double carburetors and so on. Course, that was the time of muscle cars, and I was into that, too. After that, I always wanted to build a boat and race. It was temporary insanity, but at this point it's permanent. There's no known cure." It's infectious, too; Corliss got the bug, and it was a bad case, exemplified by a bright red boat that is now a legend on the Maine coast.

The *Red Baron*, Holland 32 No. 11, went overboard in 1981. The hull had come out of the mold in 1980 and had sat around the shop nearly a year, being finished part-time. "Finally we decided we wanted to launch her and see what she'd do," says Corliss. But they almost didn't make the first race.

"The engine I was gonna race with, we couldn't get but seven cylinders to operate. We decided to put in another engine with a lot less horsepower. We started at nine in the morning, and the boys on the dock said, 'You ain't got time to get that engine changed.' I bet them we'd have her running by three in the afternoon," recalls Corliss. At five minutes to three, he fired her up.

"At that time," he says, "the Jonesporters were all using Oldsmobile engines. If you didn't have an Oldsmobile, you didn't have an engine. 'Course, I had a Ford, and they allowed as how I didn't have much chance with that. Well, she didn't only beat 'em, she slaughtered 'em," Corliss says. "She won the first boat race by eight or ten lengths, and in the second, we was so far ahead they didn't even finish; they turned off. In the next few hours, they accused me of beefing up the engine—at that time there was a 400-horsepower limit—but she was only three-twenty-five. They *knew* the Young brothers were over 400, so they weren't gonna let them race. I said, 'Let 'em race.' That's who I trounced.

"It's kinda fun, beatin' people," he says with a little smile.

At Winter Harbor, a month after that first race, the *Baron* won not only her class but the gas-engine free-for-all, as well. Since then, she has raced more years than not, with either Glenn or Corliss at the helm. "We take turns," says Glenn. "We flip a coin—whoever feels like doing it." He says it's all the boat anyway. "All you do is point it," admitting a moment later that there's more to it: "When the flag goes down, you want to be going."

And very important, of course, is the preparation work. In 1988, the night before the races, Glenn took the *Baron* down to Stonington—just to watch. "I had no intention of racing at all," he says. "She wasn't tuned up—she had just been hauling traps—and she was overheating. But everybody said, 'You got to go racing.' I listed off all that was wrong with her, and for each thing I said, someone told me, 'Oh, I'll help you with that.' We hauled her at Billings to clean the bottom, and I called my brother-in-law for the other wheel [the racing propeller]. I woke him right up out of bed, told him right where it was, and he brought it down. Damned if we didn't go out and win that year."

Usually, though, the Holland family works on the engine ahead of time. Cathy says, "Those guys can change an engine quicker than you could believe. Out and in the same day. They put the race engine in and leave it in till after the racing season's over. Then they put back the other engine." We visit the shop in mid-June, and Glenn tells us that the *Baron* is about to go under the knife. "Heart transplant," he says. "But she's used to it. Gets one a couple of times a year. We use zippers now." The engine is the primary interest of Glenn's son, Ed, though he started racing in '94 and, with his grandfather on the stern, won his first race with the *Baron*. (The rules require at least one additional person aboard a racing lobsterboat—this is known as being "on the stern," since the extra weight is always carried as far aft as possible.)

Like the rest of the family, Cathy has been involved with racing since the disease hit. "What's great about racing is that everybody does something to help. Our daughter, Andrea, has always been a part of it, and Ed is always working on the engine. I help clean, and I get the pizza. Or lots of times, I might just stay home, which is a big help—things can get very tense with too many people around."

Cathy obviously loves racing. She describes a foggy year with exhilaration: "You could hear the boats coming, but you couldn't see anything. Then, in the last race of the day, out comes the *Baron*, right out of the fog . . . " Cathy doesn't remember if the Hollands won the title that year or not, but she hasn't forgotten how she felt. She thinks that might have been the first year of the Jimmy Stevens Memorial Cup, which she's proud they won. (The trophy goes to the fastest working lobsterboat at Stonington and is given in memory of James W. Stevens, who built deck hatches, fuel tanks, and skegs for all the local builders. He died of a heart attack in 1992 at forty-nine.)

(Left to right) Glenn Holland, daughter Andrea, and father Corliss

Cathy is also proud that when their thirty-eight-footer, *Spare Parts,* raced for the first time, in 1994, she and daughter Andrea were on the stern. The boat won its class at both Stonington and Winter Harbor. "That was a historic moment for us," Cathy says. If she has anything to say about it, she'll be on the stern in the future, too. "You have to hang on when you go, but it's really fun."

In 1997, Andrea, now twenty-two, made history by being the first woman to win a sanctioned lobsterboat race. In fact, she guided the *Spare Parts* to the season class championship. Father Glenn chuckles. "I've been demoted. I'm crew chief, now."

The Hollands enjoy sharing their racing memories. Glenn tells of a year when one fellow was determined to be a length or two out in front of everyone else when the flag went down. This led to a series of false starts, when he went out early. The third time it happened, says Glenn, "I just lit right out after him and we raced on down. They were blowing horns and everything, trying to get us back, but we just kept going. The *Baron* beat him, too. They came on the radio, asking the committee if they were going to race again. 'Why bother?' one fellow said. '*Baron* beat him anyhow.'"

Corliss remembers a boat they sold to a fisherman: "'No, I'm not goin' racin',' that fellow said, but then he got it home and saw how good it went, and he changed his mind." The elder Holland is, of course, happy when his family does well, but he's just as pleased when any of the boats they built does well. "Don't matter who's drivin' it," he says.

Nonetheless, fierce competition is a fact of life in lobsterboat racing, and there's plenty of disagreement over the rules of the game. Glenn's mother, Lillian, for example, says she doesn't think it's fair for the real fishermen to have to race their working boats against the ones with the big engines—including the Holland boats.

"I don't agree with you," Corliss responds. "It's not fair for me to have to race against those little twenty-six-foot boats with the wide lifting rails." He talks of one competitor's boat in particular. "If she didn't have those on there, she'd flop right over." Corliss goes on to say how difficult it is for an outsider to win in Jonesport. He feels the rules there are set up to favor local competitors. "They don't want that cup to go anywhere but Jonesport," he says. "Well, it's been up here once already, with one of our boats [the thirty-two-foot *Twiggens*]." I heard a guy on the dock there sayin', 'The Holland's a nice boat, but you can't get a big enough wheel under 'em.' Then *Twiggens* come up through five or six lengths ahead, and I said, 'Got wheel enough now, ain't she?'"

Glenn smiles as he says, "A guy from Beals told me I was a very big thorn in their side. 'Thank you,' I said."

But, for all their enthusiasm about racing, the Hollands' link to working lobsterboats remains strong. Corliss, who is now well past seventy, fishes lobsters with the *Red Baron* in the summer, hauling a hundred traps. "I have fished more, but I don't want to work too hard," he says. "I just want to keep busy."

Glenn adds, "He doesn't haul near as many traps as some of those guys, though he said to me he'd like to put a few more in. I told him, 'You're going to make this into a job.' As is, it pays for his bait and his fuel and puts a little extra in his pocket."

"That's a good old lobsterboat," says Corliss of the *Red Baron*. "I've enjoyed that boat. I've had people wanted her, but I always say: 'No, you can't buy her.' I tell 'em, 'I'll build you one just like her. . . .'"

"Behave yourself," someone says to Corliss Holland.
"Why are people always tellin' me that?" he asks.

THE *RED BARON* Goes to San Diego

Islesboro's Ace Rolerson was visiting family in San Diego and was videotaping the America's Cup boats as they raced around the course. Suddenly, he heard his cousin say, "Now that's a beautiful boat!" But his cousin wasn't talking about one of the competitors. Ace turned to look.

There was the Maine lobsterboat *Red Baron*, flying effortlessly along the water. "All the other powerboats out there, their bows were like this," Ace angles his hand to show a blunt entry. "They were smashing through the water and hardly moving, but the *Baron* went by looking like a mirage, barely touching the water. She had her small engine in, but she was going—I swear—twenty knots, and there was just a little fine wake line behind her."

And why was the *Red Baron* in California?

In 1995, a group of Maine sailing enthusiasts put together an *America's* Cup team called PACT 95. At first dismissed by the pundits, the Maine challenge had to be taken seriously when its boat, *Young America*, turned out to be the best of the American contenders. Indeed, it was the PACT 95 boat (sailed by veteran Dennis Conner of San Diego) that ultimately defended—and lost—the cup.

From the beginning, a big fuss was made over the team's being led and supported by Mainers. When Jon Johansen, editor of the *Maine Coastal News*, saw the stars and stripes painted all over *Young America's* tender, the Newman 46 *Old Glory*, he thought it would be a good idea to send a *real* Maine lobsterboat to San Diego.

Enter Corliss Holland. Since the former boatbuilder retired, he and his wife, Lillian, or "Tiger," had headed to Florida each winter; Jon wondered if they would be willing to go to California instead and take the *Baron* with them, if their expenses were paid. "Sure, why not?" said Corliss. "I can sit just as well in California as in Florida." So, he and Tiger drove their motor home out to San Diego and waited for their boat to arrive.

"They got Dysart's, up in Bangor, to truck her out there on a flatbed," says Corliss. "They had to take the shelter house off her to get under the overpasses, but that's no problem at all; we can take it off and put it back on in half an hour when we're changing engines during race season. Only trouble was, they shrink-wrapped her, and on the way out, the wind caught the plastic and tore a hole in it and took the radar right with it. So, I didn't have radar out there. Didn't really need it."

"Sometimes you did," counters Tiger.

"Yes," agrees Corliss, "sometimes it'd be foggy, and I'd have to follow another boat in."

The *Red Baron*'s job was "doin' the weather," he explains. "We'd check the wind—the velocity and the direction—and the current. We'd go out to a buoy on the course and throw a bottle half full of water overboard and let it drift. We'd see how fast it went and in what direction. It's funny, with all that electronic equipment they had, that's how we did the current." To help the Baron in her new role, the PACT people installed a mast that was nearly as tall as the boat is long (thirty-two feet). It had an anemometer at the top, and the displays for wind speed, water depth, wind direction, boat speed, and compass heading were integrated into a single unit. Corliss wasn't wild about the mast: "I took it off 'fore I come home," he says. "I wouldn't have my boat come into Belfast with that on it!"

Corliss and his crew reported to the rest of the team on a scrambled cell phone, "so the other side couldn't understand what we were sayin'," he explains. "We were losin' a lot of those phones overboard. The fellow would stand on the washboard [side deck] and lay a phone down on the house top. Then the boat'd roll, and over it'd go. Some expensive, but I didn't care—it wasn't my equipment.

"We'd do the weather right up till about ten minutes before the start," remembers Corliss. "Then we'd run up to the line and watch the race. I always had spectators—sometimes three or four, never more than eight. We'd follow along as they raced. Course, we had to stay outside the perimeter; you couldn't get too close.

"It was rough all the time. Had to go out through a couple of jetties, and the wind would be southerly, blowin' in, and the tide'd be runnin' out—you knew it'd be rough."

"Tell about the first day, when I went with you," Tiger says.

"Well, Dave Dysart and his truck drivers wanted a ride. She come, too. We shouldn't have gone out—we scared her 'bout half to death. Comin' back in, the bow'd be right down when a wave would come up underneath the stern—she didn't push her bow under, but we were surfin'." Tiger wouldn't go out on the *Baron* again for a month. "They had a spectator boat 130-odd feet long," says Corliss, "and *she* almost broached. That's how bad the waves were.

"Got so I'd get out in the morning and drive onto the jetty for a look, and sometimes I'd tell them, 'It's too rough, I'm not goin' out. If you want to go, I'll see you when you get back.'" More than once, the Cup contenders would proceed to the course, but the race would end up being called off. Corliss recalls, "Got so Joel, on *Old Glory*, would say, 'We probably just ought to ask you, Corliss, before we go out. We'd save a lot of time bangin' around out there if we did.'

Tucked among the yachts at a San Diego marina, the **Red Baron** *looks proud but out of place.*

"I had a young lady with me one time, and she was sittin' back in the stern. She was seasick—had her head in a plastic bag the whole time she was out there. I said, 'You know, I think we better take her in or she's gonna die.' So we did, and when we got in, I asked her how she liked the trip. She said it was really interesting. Well, I guess it was, her head in that bag all the time.

"There was a woman from Miami, a photographer, and she wanted to know if I had a head on board. 'I got a five-gallon pail, right down there,' I told her. But she held it. The good thing about that head is it flushes every time.

Corliss recalls that the San Diego Yacht Club used Bayliners—mass-produced fiberglass runabouts—to police the spectator fleet. "It used to get boring sometimes, and I'd play with those Bayliners. I'd work my way inside the perimeter and get those fellows to chase me out. One time I was over to the San Diego Yacht Club at a party, and they introduced me all around. One of those people was in charge of the Bayliners. 'You're that son of a gun who's always playing with me?' he asked."

"One time they were doing an interview on the dock right behind my boat, and the people were all dressed up nice. I'd just fueled up, and with full tanks, the *Baron* puts her exhaust pipes under the water. 'You want to see some fun?' I asked Joel. 'You ain't got the nerve,' he said, and that's all it took. I hit the starter and she blowed that water out about twenty feet—soaked 'em in good shape. The big shots come down to give me hell, but they got laughing so hard they couldn't do it. I pulled the same trick one time here at the town landing—knocked a guy right off his sailboat into the water. 'Oh, 'd I do that?' I asked him. 'It's a miracle you've lived as long as you have,' the boys down there said to me.

"I'm not a sailboat man, by any means," admits Corliss, "but we did see some beautiful sailing, specially the tacking duels. How the devil they ever got by without runnin' into each other I don't know. Specially at the buoys. We would be right close to them at the buoys.

"I knew *New Zealand* was gonna win. They wanted me to go over and get a look at her one time, at her sails and everything. I had to run my engine much faster to stay up with her. I told 'em, 'You may win this one, but they're gonna get the Cup.'"

The *Baron* wasn't actually the only Maine lobsterboat in San Diego. Besides her and *Old Glory*, there were three commercial boats (two Duffy & Duffy models and a Young Brothers' 30) and a pleasure boat that Corliss thinks might have been a Newman. He never saw her out. "There's an awful lot of boats there, but they don't use them much," he says. The Young Brothers' 30 belonged to the Coast Guard; Corliss doesn't know what they used her for. "They come up alongside me, and the fellow said he bought her because he really wasn't interested in speed. I told him, 'Well, you did just fine, because you haven't got it.'"

The Duffys fished for spiny lobsters, a very different species from the one that ends up in Maine traps. Corliss was going to try a West Coast lobster "just to see if I liked 'em, but I never got the courage up." Most of the other lobsterboats in San Diego were outboards, he says. "Ninety percent of the time, you'd see somebody towing them in. If I was goin' to fish out there, I'd want something reliable—the only lee you've got is the Hawaiian Islands."

The *Red Baron* attracted a lot of attention. "Everybody in the world wanted to see her, wanted to ride on her," says Corliss. "More than on *Old Glory*, matter of fact. Joel wanted me to race him, but I said it was a waste of time. I could beat him, and the engine wouldn't even breathe hard."

When the Cup trials were finished, Corliss said, "Now's the time to get the hell out of here and do some serious racin'." He was home in Maine for the first lobsterboat races of the season. But he's glad he went to California. "It really was an interesting trip. I'm glad I had the chance. I'd go to New Zealand, if they wanted to pay my way."

"You'll be goin' alone," says Tiger, though perhaps she'd reconsider if the offer came. They don't think it will.

Corliss Holland enjoyed his trip west but prefers Maine.

TOM HUGHES, *WALDO INDEPENDENT*

After the *America's* Cup races were over, the PACT 95 training boat *Spirit of Unum* was shipped back to Maine and fitted out in Camden. We stopped to chat with one of the crewmen as he worked on her sails on the dock; he was perfunctory in his answers to questions we asked about the team and the *America's* Cup boats, and he kept on about his business. We were obviously a nuisance. Then I told him I was writing about lobsterboats. He showed a little interest: "Oh?"

"I was hoping to get something from one of you guys about the *Red Baron*," I said.

There was a total change of expression. He stood up and looked me in the eye. "Oh, we loved having her out there! It was special of Corliss to give us his time like that. I never got to go on her—I was always on the support boat. But I loved seeing her—I got some pictures of her running wide open. A beautiful boat."

"My house is a mess, my truck is a mess, but my boat's pretty good. You never know when you'll find a pretty girl who'd like to go for a ride—you don't want her to stick when she sits down."

—Gweeka Williams, Vinalhaven

GWEEKA WILLIAMS
Builds a New Boat

It's late March. The Hollands meet us at the door of their Belfast shop; they're on their way to Castine to pick up their son at the Maritime Academy, but they direct us to Vinalhaven's Gweeka Williams, who is sitting on a block of wood under a shiny new black hull, sanding. Two or three other men are working on a Holland 38 farther back in the shop.

Gweeka is a strong-looking man in his forties with strikingly bright blue eyes. He wears a grubby black baseball cap that says *Pirates Cove, Matinicus*. Richard Williams doesn't know the derivation of his nickname but remembers no time that he wasn't called Gweeka. "Everybody on Vinalhaven has names like that. Probably there's the best collection of nicknames out there of anywhere I've been. I got more than that one. Some of them aren't nice."

"I do a lot with lobsterboats," he says. "Build 'em, fish 'em, race 'em." This new boat replaces his old *Illusion*, a fifteen-year-old Holland 32 that he sold this winter. "The guy wanted it in December, but I didn't want the income last year, so I made him wait till January 1." Masking tape spells out *Shamu* on the new boat's bow; it's an appropriate name for the black hull with its white bottom. "We got a phantom taper here, comes around weekends and tapes names on things," says Gweeka. He won't tell us the real name of his boat. "Bad luck," he explains.

The hull is a Holland 32, but it has the keel of a 38 to allow a bigger propeller. This keel, though, is about half as thick as a normal one. Gweeka tells us to feel the seam; he has 'glassed it so you can't feel the break at all. He is sanding the skeg and works on it for two hours as he talks. "We changed a few

133

other things—toyed with the run of the bottom a little bit, some other little things," he says. Gweeka explains that the *Illusion* had lifting rails, but he states, "This boat won't need 'em—there ain't gonna be much left in the water. Air rails, if anything.

"This boat is gonna be my baby. My other one I kinda let go, and I feel kinda bad. That boat was some good to me. So far, the guy that's got it is taking real good care of it.

Gweeka Williams

"I finished the *Illusion* at my uncle's shop on Vinalhaven. He built wooden boats. I used to work with him, and I like working with wood. He thought fiberglass is radioactive; he was scared of it. 'Glass is different—you do everything backwards," he says, referring to the necessity of starting with the outside of the boat and working in as the hull is laid up in the mold. " 'Course, boatbuilders are all crazier than hell anyway. They all build boats the right way, and you don't know shit—that's what they think. One time I was in the shop with my uncle, and he had a boat almost done. Corliss Holland came to visit. 'Well, cap'n,' my uncle asks, 'What do you think?' "

" 'Well, cap'n, you do it all wrong,' says Corliss.

"You could just see my uncle bristling. 'What do you mean?' he says.

" 'Christ, we paint our boats before we build 'em.'

" 'Well,' says my uncle, 'I don't pour my boats out of a five-gallon bucket.' But they was both Masons, so everything smoothed over."

Gweeka says he fishes hard. "I fish a thousand traps. I finish up between Christmas and the first or second of January, then I put up my gear, and I stop. I usually have a project—last winter I built a new kitchen, a new bedroom and bath—and I'd been thinkin' about a new boat. So this slot came up, and here I am.

"Usually I start fishin' again in the middle or the beginning of April. This year I'll be late, because this boat won't go in till the first of May. But they're already startin' out there—everybody does that when spring starts comin'. There's a few warm days, and you smell mud and think, Jeez, gotta get them traps over." Gweeka says he's fortunate that his family has a dock; five men fish from it currently, and they can store their gear on the waterfront. "Makes a big difference, to have your traps right there. You see these houses way inland, with piles of traps outside, and you know how they all got there—truckload by truckload. But Vinalhaven is still a fishing town. There's some who don't want it to be, but it is, and you can keep your traps in the town parking lot—makes it a lot easier for people."

Gweeka says there are 250 full-time fishermen on Vinalhaven. "There's quite a few go scallopin', wintertime, or shrimpin', and there's a lot of them in that 'green gold'—urchins ain't seemed to drop off out there. You still catch a lot of them in lobster traps. I got probably ten pounds of spines in each hand." Gweeka says the beauty of Vinalhaven is that it's as far offshore as it is. "That's why there's still urchins. You get the wrong kind of weather, you can get stuck out there." Gweeka calls Penobscot Bay "our moat."

Vinalhaven is not a place anyone from off-island would want to start lobstering. "Some fool tries it every once in a while, but there's a lot of 'razor bottom' out there," he says; Vinalhaven fishermen are as protective of their territory as anyone on the coast. Gweeka says it's not hard for a local youngster to start, however, "if he works hard and ain't too bad a crook." He explains, "Fishin' is all there is to do—there's only so much plumbing, electrician work. You can paint houses or roll out red carpets for rich people, but mostly it's fishin'. A lot of young people are moving away—but not so many that it's a problem. It ain't gonna die out."

Gweeka has been living in Belfast while he works on his new boat. "This is the longest I've lived off the island since I was in the service, twenty-five years ago. It's different—you can get in your car and go somewhere—but all I do is go to Rockland and take the ferry," he says. "I used to get traveling fever every two or three years, and go to California or the Bahamas or wherever, but I'd get there and just want to come back. I don't even bother no more.

"A lot of guys—after they've been at it a long time—have their houses and their boats all paid for, and their kids are all growed up. So, they go to Florida for the winter. If they got a little extra money, they can do that. But if you're into lobsterboat racin', you don't have any extra money. Period. You can make a living and eat, or go racin' and starve." He chuckles, "I can stand to lose a few pounds."

"The whole deal is racin'," says Gweeka. "I sold the *Illusion*, a perfectly good lobsterboat and not a bad racin' boat either, and here I am settin' on the cement floor, sandin' my fingerprints away." We ask if the *Illusion* will be racing this year. "Christ, that'd be something, if he beat me. Might get me out of this business once and for all.

"This engine is a wicked gamble. Nobody else has one. It's right over there under that sheet with the ducks on it," Gweeka tells us, pointing to a spot beside the boat's port bow. It's a huge engine, shiny blue with chrome trim, built in Florida by Daytona, a custom engine company. "Pretty, ain't it?" asks Gweeka. "I paid more for it than for my house. I've got an acre and a half of land and a hundred feet of deep frontage, but that engine cost more.

"God, ain't that awful! Six races, two minutes apiece—$30,000 for twelve minutes a year. Actually, $31,776, to be exact. That's only up to this point, and I ain't even started yet. But it looks good, costs good, oughta be good. I don't see how it could possibly fail—it might, but I'll sulk the rest of my life if it does. And I can sulk good, too. But I've got an idea she's gonna be fast.

"This boat weighs about half what my old one did—you can just about walk over to her and pick her up. The old boat was stock—a little light for her time, but a dinosaur compared to technology today. Like the difference between a wood-and-canvas airplane and a new aluminum one. But light don't necessarily mean weak, with the materials you got today. You put your knees and girders and everything that bears weight in the right places—hell, light don't amount to nothin' any more."

We ask about choosing the right propeller for an unknown engine and boat pair. Basically, every propeller is identified by its diameter and its "pitch," which is the theoretical horizontal distance it would travel in one revolution. "It's kind of like a stab in the dark," Gweeka says. "This [hull/keel/engine] has never been done before, so we've talked and talked and talked and talked about it. We came to a happy medium—we hope we did—but basically it's a stab in the dark. The wheel's a 26-inch [diameter] by 34-inch [pitch]. You can have pitch put in, which we hope, or taken out, which we don't hope, and then you can put some cup in the blades. But it ain't like a bag of golf clubs, where you reach in and get what you like."

Glenn Holland has a bunch of different wheels on hand for the *Red Baron* or any normal 32, but Gweeka's boat is a totally new configuration, and propellers this size are expensive. "Say the engine's supposed to turn at 2,800," says Gweeka. "If it goes 3,000, you give the wheel a little more pitch. If it's then at 2,900, you give it another little *tunk,* and when it's at 2,800, you can start the fine-tuning.

"I'm having a rudder made you can shave with. Stainless steel. Wes Shute has one—he almost killed himself putting his wheel on. He did get cut." (The next time we visit, the rudder is in place. It's shiny and very sharp on the leading edge, to minimize drag. "It's really too pretty; it ought to be on my fireplace at home," says Gweeka. "But I do have a hole I can look down at it through." He has built in a well, or access port, so he can get at his propeller from the cockpit in case it should get fouled.)

"I hope to get to all the races this year," says Gweeka. "Last year I only got to one. I worked real hard—my brother got in a mess and couldn't go fishing, so I had to tend his traps. He hit a weird sea, he went over, and his boat ran over him two or three times. Pretty near cut off his leg."

Gweeka, himself, has never fallen victim to a serious fishing accident, but he's seen the hard side of making a living on the water. When he was young and only had a twenty-foot outboard, he fished Vinalhaven in the good weather and went sternman a couple of winters with a friend on Matinicus. "That's a lonesome piece of real estate in the wintertime," he says. "Come spring, the pegs will fall right over in the cribbage board, and you've played poker so much you can't read the dates on your pennies. And there's no law out there."

Gweeka has fished Vinalhaven in the winters, too. "Where you gotta go, you're running outside. The sea acts different in the winter, and it's cold. And if the ship's gonna break down, it's gonna do it then. You got no daylight, and it's always rough. You've got competition with the scallop draggers and the shrimpers, and they're gettin' your traps. You go out and get a hundred pounds of lobsters at six or seven dollars a pound, you got a bunch of money in your pocket, you feel good. But then in the spring, you've lost all that equipment, and your boat's all beat to hell, and your skiff's all stove up. I give that up six or seven years ago. I've hauled till my nose bled every day till Christmas already, and I'd just as soon sit underneath a boat and sand," he says, doing just that.

If there are 200 lobstermen, Gweeka says, there'll be 200 ways of doing a job, and they'll all be right. "Everybody does the same thing different," he says. The one thing they all agree about is the Coast Guard. Gweeka lists all the operating expenses facing him: his trap tags, license, boat registration, VHF license, insurance. "And then you got to have all this junk the Coast Guard makes you pile up even though you'll never use it."

He had a discussion with an inspector about his life ring, which he keeps below. It's supposed to be in the cockpit, for quick access; there, however, it's in the way, it'll weather, the attached line will rot, and the fisherman will just have to replace it. But that's where the law says it must be. " 'Finest kind,' I told him, 'but if I'm out alone, who's gonna throw it to me?' " He notes that the yachtsman may need lots of safety equipment—even though, ironically, he's not required to carry it—but the lobster fisherman doesn't. "He has his buddies out there," says Gweeka.

Even in relatively minor ways, the lobstermen are aware of each other. One time, he says, he was late going out after waiting for the bait man to come. "I have to steam seven miles to my traps," says Gweeka, "so when finally I got my bait, I felt like I had to rush, and I put it right to her. The gaff just fell right off the washboard, but I didn't see it. Seven miles later, I got to my first trap and saw the gaff's gone. I tried usin' my scrub brush, but it broke off. I tried drivin' a nail in somethin', and that broke off, too. Just about then, the radio squawks, '*Illusion*, you missin' somethin?' I had the gaff painted Day-Glo so you could see it, and he'd found it right there in the harbor. I was lucky: I met him halfway in; he was comin' out my way anyway.

"The boat costs $150,000, and gaffs cost about three, but you couldn't possibly have a spare one," says Gweeka. "You got spare bait bags, a spare lobster measure, spare this and spare that, but no spare gaff. Sunglasses, too. I've lost more sunglasses on the mooring. You know, you lean over to pick up the buoy, and *foop*, there they go. I pulled the mooring up once and there was seven thousand pairs of sunglasses on it.

"Plenty of lobstermen wouldn't tell you this, but a lotta times you miss your buoy the first pass. You miss it the second time, that's good for a three-star fit right there, and if your sternman laughs, well, that's the worst. The primary instruction for anyone on my boat is 'don't laugh.' You can sit there and chuckle, but don't laugh."

Our conversation drifts back to boatbuilding. "Smell that wood," says Gweeka. One of the other men in the shop is sawing a strip of wood trim. "Cherry. One thing I miss not building the wooden boats is that wood smell. I'd like to build a wooden boat, and maybe I will, someday. But you got to set in a boatyard a couple of weeks every spring, diggin' and scratchin' and paintin' on that boat. I kinda like it, it's kinda fun—but not having to do it is a pretty good time, too. If you feel like coddling a 'glass boat, you can get a can of wax and go at it."

When we return to the Holland shop several weeks later, Gweeka is sanding again. He has trimmed his windows with teak (he had to have *some* wood), and he has installed bronze chocks and a big shiny bronze bitt on the bow. We remark on the bitt. "Ain't that a corker?" asks Gweeka. "That's impulse buyin' at its finest." Gweeka had an old-fashioned wooden fitting on his old boat but says, "I was gonna build me another, till I happened to walk by that one on the shelf up at Hamilton's. It was cryin', 'Buy me, buy me!' "

The boat's exhaust pipe is impressive too: stainless steel, it measures six inches in diameter with an angled-back tip at the top. "She's gotta breathe," says Gweeka, "and she'll prob'ly breathe me right into court. Four-thirty in the morning, I love to go on down through the Thorofare and blow the shingles right off some of them cottages. I had a real good time one night. I was at the Black Pearl in Rockland with a friend, and we'd had a few but we wasn't drunk—well, maybe we was drunk, but I've been drunker.

"Anyway, they asked us to leave—said we looked like we might get rowdy. We wasn't doin' nothin', but they thought we *might* get noisy. Christ sake, that's no way to treat anybody. I was a regular customer there, and that's how they treated me. 'Finest kind,' I said, 'by Jesus, they want to hear some noise, we'll give 'em some noise.' You know how the Black Pearl is, out on pilings? Well, I took the *Illusion* right under the Black Pearl. She had two straight pipes, no tipbacks or nothin', and we ran back and forth underneath there for about fifteen minutes, till the cops came. Then we took off.

"Next mornin', four o'clock, I went out to go fishin' as usual. The minute I reached for my key, a big spotlight come on me. There's a fish warden in a big patrol boat. Wasn't he mad! 'You realize how early I had to get up to come get you?' he says. 'I've had complaints about you all summer long, here in Vinalhaven, and I've turned my head, let you go. But now you're goin' to Rockland; that's enough.' He wouldn't let me go till I got mufflers, so I went up to Belfast and borrowed a couple from Glenn. Christ, that's the earliest that warden ever got up in his life.

"But it was some beautiful, how she fit right under those pilings there. Didn't she bark! Had a 460 Lincoln in her. I liked that engine best, but prob'ly the best engine really is the one that's in her now, an 8.2 diesel. Jeez, that's a wicked engine for haulin' traps. Haul all day long for fifteen or twenty bucks. They sold it to me wicked cheap, to race it for 'em. They had some trouble with those engines, but I never had problems with it. I did have to replace the head once, but that's nothin'—I knew that was gonna happen. I cooked her—I knew she was gettin' hot, but I didn't bother to stop. I had four first-place races with that diesel."

Gweeka is a month late on his projected launch date on the new boat. "I got no one to blame but myself," he says, adding, "This is the boat nobody has nothin' for—the *Misfit* ought to be her name. I thought Vinalhaven was the only place you couldn't get nothin', but Belfast is just as bad.

"I'm gettin' anxious about goin' home—everyone's workin' out there. I'm gonna have to have a shoehorn to get my traps in." Gweeka would like to be working—and he's got to be ready for the first races in the end of June. I ask how he'll get the boat tuned up. Gweeka says the radar gun is the key. "You can go out, and *boom*, you know just what you're doin'. Then you can change somethin' and see if you're doin' better or worse. It also tells what the other guys are doin'," which is why Gweeka refers to the gun as "the lie detector."

When we stop by the shop another day, Corliss, Glenn, and Gweeka are on coffee break. It's spring, so everyone's thinking about racing. They're swapping stories. That they all know these tales already makes no difference to anyone's enjoyment. They talk of one competitor who often comes by to see what they're up to. "He's due here most any time," Glenn says. "We lie to him. Well, we don't lie, we just don't tell him the whole truth. He came in here one time, said his boat was clocked at forty-seven, and asked how fast we were. We said, 'Oh, a little over forty.' Funny how our forty-two-mile-per-hour boat could beat his forty-seven."

The classes in which the boats compete used to vary from race to race, but everyone understands that you want to be the smallest in your class. Glenn is talking. "They used to cut 'em off at thirty-two feet. The *Baron* is thirty-two feet three inches. 'You sell her as a 32, don't you?' they asked me. I said, 'Well, yes, I do, but she's thirty-two feet three inches.' Weren't they unhappy! Then they changed it to thirty-three feet. All those Young Brothers' 33s, they didn't want to race us. Well, I don't blame them. I don't like having to race against all those small boats, the twenty-eight footers and all. I wonder how small they'll get 'em."

But even if the Hollands had to race the *Spare Parts,* Glenn's 38-footer, against Gweeka's new boat, that would be all right. "I can't lose, if either of us wins," Glenn says. The Hollands don't care what boat finishes first, as long as it's a Holland.

"We might be first and second," suggests Gweeka.

"Or we might tie for first. That'd be good, cost them some money—they'd have to get another trophy." Glenn laughs. "I could ask you for the Grey Poupon as we cross the line. That'd be good."

"Yuh," says Gweeka, "like that time my engine was about 240, and we were out in front, and I said, 'We might as well have a couple of beers.' So we cruised on down there and crossed the line ahead of everybody, drinkin' beers."

Glenn remembers a race where his engine was getting very hot. His sternman asked him what they were going to do. "I looked at the engine, I looked at the Young brothers behind me, and I looked at the finish line. 'Let her burn,' I said."

"Remember when you used that airplane fuel, down there in Portland?" Gweeka asks Glenn.

"She barked some, but didn't she like that!"

"You talk about makin' an engine happy," says Gweeka. "She was smilin' from valve cover to valve cover!"

"You know, it's funny," says Glenn. "Before a race, you're all nervous, your stomach's just a churnin', you can't stand, you can't sit, you can't do nothin' but worry, and then when you get to the line, you're just as solid as a rock."

"There was that time you tossed your cookies," Gweeka reminds him.

"I did, literally," admits Glenn. "Cathy'd given me a lunch; I don't know why—I can't eat anything before a race anyway. The bag with a sandwich and some cookies and whatnot was settin' on the dash. Well, when I hit the throttle, a toolbox just flew back and wiped out that bag. There were cookies everywhere. That plastic bag was just floating in the air, and I was sure it was gonna get sucked into the carburetor."

"Well," says Gweeka, "the toolbox actually stayed put. The boat went out from under it."

"That's right, and then when the boat went by, the stern caught that box and brought it along."

A $30,000 custom-built engine propels Gweeka's thirty-two-foot **Bad Penny** *into the lead.*

BANGOR DAILY NEWS

"Remember when they were squeezin' you that time?" asks Gweeka.

"Oh, they'll squeeze you, hopin' you're gonna back off the throttle some, but I think, Just come on over, come right aboard if you want to."

"That time, I could've just reached over and handed them a beer," Gweeka says.

The stories could go on all afternoon, but there's work to be done, and everyone wanders off to different corners of the shop. Gweeka turns his attention back to his behind-schedule boat.

Just six days before the Boothbay races, Gweeka launched his boat. Her stern sported shiny gold letters: *Bad Penny.* More than once during that week, she was hauled and put back in, and Gweeka made fifty-mile trips to one shop or another, tweaking the propeller. Finally, the *Bad Penny* headed to Boothbay.

In the class for diesels of 376 to 500 horsepower, she crossed the line well ahead of her competitors. The free-for-all diesel race was close, with ten boats starting and three going down the course side-by-side, within inches of one another. It was hard to see who won, but the radio announced the results, First Place: *Bad Penny.*

Gweeka lost the Fastest Lobsterboat race, which was open to the top-placing diesels and gas-powered boats. Corliss Holland and the *Red Baron* took first in a squeaker over the twenty-eight-foot *Little Jan.*

"I'm gonna have a thirty-eight-footer when I grow up," Gweeka says. But he's in no hurry to stop racing his new boat. After all, Corliss still competes, and he's seventy-three now. "He ain't grown up yet," says Gweeka. "I guess I don't need to worry about it for a while."

Lobsterboat Superstitions

A lot of fishermen have superstitions. Lynn Wessel says her husband, Steve, believes you should never fish a blue boat. Apparently, Steve's brother David bought a used boat, and his wife painted it an electric blue. Lynn explains, "David blew two engines, and everything went wrong. It was his worst year ever. Steve told his brother, 'For God's sake, repaint the boat.'"

"Once they put her back to buff, everything was all right," Steve says.

The fear of blue extends beyond hull color. Gweeka Williams of Vinalhaven tells of his Uncle Philo, who ordered a new Osco Ford engine. It arrived on the ferry. Gweeka recalls, "They got that engine offloaded, and by God it was blue. Uncle Philo wouldn't get near it. They said they'd send him over a couple cans of spray paint, but no way would Uncle Philo touch that thing." So the engine went back to Rockland, where it was painted green. "After that, no matter what, them Osco Ford engines was painted Vinalhaven Green before they come out. Said right on the invoice, 'Vinalhaven Green,' $25."

It's a common belief among fishermen that if you whistle aboard a boat, the wind will start to blow. Steve Wessel was out hauling one day with a new helper. "I knew a wind was going to come up," he says. "I could tell by the sky. When little pieces of cloud are breaking away, my grandfather used to say, 'They're passing out handbills.' So I told this guy, 'Whatever you do, don't whistle, it'll bring up a wind.' So the guy whistled, and we hit a freak wave, and it just soaked him. He was ashen white. Then the wind come on, and didn't it scream. He's a believer, now," Steve says, "but I knew it'd happen."

Not all fishermen, however, subscribe to the traditional superstitions. "They say you should never whistle on a boat," says Gweeka, "but Christ, it

143

always blows anyway." He notes that pigs are supposed to be bad luck, but recalls, "Henry Gross had a mast on his boat, and he cut a big pig outa plywood, and put it up on the mast like a weathervane. He'd whistle and watch the pig swing around and around."

But, the pig issue is very important to some. Avery Kelley tells with a gleam in his eye about an old fellow who lived on Beals Island near Pig Island Gut. This fisherman believed that saying the word "pig" on a boat brought terrible luck. "Some of the guys would see him out there, and they'd call him up on the radio and ask him where he was," says Avery. "He'd answer without thinkin', 'Pig Island Gut,' and then he'd get all upset, sayin', 'Oh no, I said the word, I said the word!' He'd be all worked up, stutterin' and all."

"Some guys won't say the word 'pig' on a boat, or even 'pork'," Lynn Wessel says. "I did the shopping when we went offshore, and one time I was cooking pork chops when this terrible gale came up out of nowhere. Steve insists it was because I had pork."

There are a number of superstitions about boat names. For example, Gweeka wouldn't divulge the name of his new boat until he absolutely had to; though this superstition isn't universal, he knows other people who feel the same way. And to many, including Steve Wessel, it's terrible luck to change a boat's name. "Steve's other boat was named for his first wife," says Lynn. "He told me, 'I'll change it, if you want,' but I said, 'Oh no, it's fine with me.' When we sold the *Misty Lynn,* the next owner didn't change her name. Then he sold it—we sold it for him—to a guy in Rhode Island. He was going to change the name, but Steve told him it was bad luck, and he never did."

"I'm kinda fussy about my superstitions," says Gweeka. "Some bother me, some don't. I don't care about launching on Fridays, but my uncle was real upset by that. I built my first boat in his shop, and I was all set to put her over on Friday. He stood right in the way and said, 'You ain't gonna launch this boat today,' and I said, 'By God I am, if I have to throw you overboard!'

"You're not supposed to start a voyage on a Friday, either," adds Gweeka. "A lot of that stuff I ain't superstitious about, but some of it I am—wicked. You should never turn hatch covers upside down, *never.* And never put the oars in your skiff backwards, with the fans ahead." There are some new superstitions, too, Gweeka explains. "Like the ferry. You should never pop your beer before the boat leaves. You can have it in your hand, but don't open it.

"And you better pay your income tax on time. You make your own bad luck if you don't," he says. He speaks from experience.

"Uncle Alvin was gettin' on in age, and he'd built up his boatbuilding business for his son. He took a lot of pride in what he done. But then his son died young—forty he was. Well, Uncle Alvin, he mourned, and he didn't want to go to the shop any more. After a month or two, he was gettin' on his wife's nerves, and finally one day, when he was awful depressed, she said to him, 'Alvin, is there any way you could build a little boat just the way you built a big one?'

" 'I guess there's no reason you couldn't,' said Uncle Alvin, and there wasn't much else said. But pretty soon he was missing. By-and-by, she looked out, and he was in the shop—zip by the window, zip by again. He come back and put the teakettle on for steam, but he was gettin' on with the project, and she didn't want to say much.

"Once he'd started and had built one of them little boats, everyone just tortured him to death wanting more. One guy asked for a Friendship sloop. Well, pretty soon a sloop went through the Reach, and Uncle Alvin watched her go by. He said, 'I studied her pretty good,' and he built that little Friendship sloop. Then someone wanted a torpedo-stern lobsterboat, and he made some of them. They put chainsaw motors in them and radio control. Weren't they nice little boats!"

—Avery Kelley, Beals Island

WILLIS BEAL
A Link to a Boatbuilding Tradition

Richard Pinkham and Eugene Robinson of RP Boat Shop in Steuben did something that many boatbuilders before them wished they'd been able to do: they convinced Willis Beal to design a lobsterboat for production in fiberglass. "It was quite a job to get him to do it," says Richard. "He'd always worked in wood. When he puts two pieces of wood together, they're together. It's like they growed together.

"He'd been approached by four other boatbuilders—we just happened to hit him at the right time on the right spot, and he built a beautiful boat for us.

145

He's got a design that come out of himself. It was within him, not something that come out of a computer."

Willis Beal ties the whole lobsterboat story together. He's the last of the Beals Island wooden-lobsterboat builders, he built two torpedo-stern models, and he designed what may be the biggest fiberglass thirty-five-footer yet. Some say the new boat is ugly, with its straight lines, and fussy in the water, but it's selling well, and the men who fish the boat love it. It can carry 200 traps, where thirty-five-footers built in the 1960s carried 115 or 120, and it's a stable platform to work from. In fact, this model epitomizes the recent direction of lobsterboat design. Willis raced his own RP-35 in the dragger class at Jonesport this year and crossed the finish line well ahead of his competition. The boat kicked up a lot of water, but she moved out.

Willis admires one of Alvin Beal's "little boats," an early, open model.

BANGOR DAILY NEWS

There weren't any boatbuilders in Willis Beal's direct ancestry, but even as a youngster he was intrigued by the trade. "Both my grandfathers were fishermen," he says. "My father was handy with tools and all, but he never ever built a boat." Willis recalls that as a kid, he'd run off and watch the local builders at work: "Alvin Beal was a real nice man. He built my father a boat back in '55; that's when I first got to know him. As I got interested in building boats, I visited his shop; he was a real good friend, helped me a lot.

Fishing appealed to young Willis, too, primarily because his father was a fisherman. The elder Beal lobstered and tended two herring weirs at Roque Island. "While I was growing up, I fished with him summers at different times till I went out on my own, and of course after that when he needed me." After he had trouble with his back, Willis's father had to quit, and for sixteen years thereafter he worked as superintendent on Roque Island, where there was a year-round farm. "Then he went back in the boat with me—his back had healed up by then," Willis says. "We enjoyed each other's company, and he was a big help to me. Sixteen years he went with me.

"I used to get done fishing the last of November, then I went into the boatshop and didn't get out till August sometimes, or even September," says Willis. "I built two boats each year with my father-in-law. He worked with me twenty years. Then I went to just one boat a year. It's quite a job to work on two boats and mend your traps and your gear; I found out I wasn't Superman.

"When I was getting started, Freddy Lenfestey helped me a lot. I worked with him the winter of 1963 when he was building a boat for my father, and we repaired another one. We were good friends. He was a real talented man— he could do anything—fix motors, sharpen saws, paint lettering, carve. He carved decoys and painted them, and he made a replica of the Budweiser team with the dog on it and the whole works. They found out about it and came down and offered him $10,000 for it. 'What would I need $10,000 for?' he asked them.

"There were several other builders here, so if I needed to know anything, I could ask them and they'd tell me and I could count on what they told me," says Willis. "I counted on Alvin a lot for that torpedo. If I weren't sure about something, I'd go ask him. Before he started on his own, he had worked with several people who had built those boats. He built ninety-seven boats of different kinds—lobsterboats and pleasure boats.

"Harold Gower, he was real good to me. And I worked with Clinton Beal three different winters—I think I helped him build four boats. I learned a lot from him—anything I wanted to know, he'd tell me or show me. He really got me started. I knew what a boat should look like, and most of the time I knew what I had to do to get it that way. Sometimes, though, you need a little help to get going.

"My mother was a teacher," says Willis, "close to thirty years. She was hoping I'd do the same, but I wanted to get outside and work with my hands." When he was nine years old, Willis and his brother Robert, then six, fished twenty traps together from a rowing skiff. "He did the rowing, I did the hauling. He wanted to haul, but he wasn't strong enough. Then we got a bigger skiff and an outboard. That's how a lot of guys started out. They worked up." Now Robert teaches in the elementary school in Jonesport. "He's taught twenty-six years so far," says Willis. "He has always fished summer and early fall, till the time changes, but he's thinking of retiring and going fishing full time."

Willis says fishing is easier than building boats. "There's no harder work than boatbuilding, specially in wood. You're always on your hands and knees crawling around and lifting and pushing on something, working at a disadvantage. Then you have all the dust. As far as I'm concerned, though, fiberglass is worse, what with the odor and all. My boat's the only 'glass one I've finished off, and in fact, if I could've afforded to get someone to do it for me, I would have. I guess the Lord was good to me, because he let me get it done without getting sick, and I enjoyed the challenge of it. But I couldn't taste anything or smell anything until I got out fishing again. I don't believe it's healthy stuff to work with. I'm getting too old for that. I might be driven to it, but I don't want to. I've shown I can do it."

Another Beals Island lobsterboat takes shape in Willis's shop. Typically, she's fine forward and flat aft.

Willis Beal has built twenty-six wooden boats and is admired by many as one of the finest builders in the country. He takes pride in having taken the extra steps to make sure his boats would last. Willis explains: "All splices are done with red lead or wood preservative before they're put together—in the keel, the stem, the stern frame. And the rabbet line and the limber holes are all done with preservative before the planks or timbers are put on. Most would put them down on bare wood and then preserve just what they can see."

He also takes special care with the sharp risers—the heavy transverse frames that are sawed and shaped to fit the curves of the hull. (By contrast, ribs are lighter, and they're steamed, then bent into place.) "I make the sharp risers of two-inch-thick oak set on edge, cut as deep as I can make them," explains Willis. "The shallowest are ten inches and they get up over twenty. I top them out and put the floor beams over them, instead of on a stringer. That gives a lot of weight, but a lot of strength, too. They're spaced about every twenty inches apart, stem to stern. They're all bolted down into the keel—it gives a lot of strength. When the boat's just planked, you can walk on it and see it move, but you put those in, and it's all done moving."

Willis built three cabin cruisers, all on the lobsterboat model. "One was forty feet long by thirteen feet, ten inches wide. That was a big task for me—possibly the most challenging other than the torpedoes—because it was all finished off in mahogany, dressed right up. It was a big job. I got it done the last part of September and had two or three people helping me at a time. I had to oversee the whole thing, plan the whole thing, and do all the ordering.

"I tried to do as much of the building as I could," he says, "but I had to get help. There was 6,000 hours in it, and I put in 3,800 of those myself. I played myself out. After I got my traps out, it was two months till I got back to myself. It's unbelievable just the wiring in a boat like that—all hidden, none of it exposed. Then there's the plumbing—hot and cold running water—refrigeration, galley stove, and all that.

The fiberglass RP 35 that Willis designed breaks with local tradition in its broad beam and high sides.

"One of those cabin cruisers was for the Gardiners down on Roque Island—they've sold that boat, and it went to the Caribbean. So you never know where they're gonna end up. The first cabin cruiser I built went to New York, and now she belongs to a doctor up here, in Lincolnville.

"The biggest boat was a forty-one-footer; she's fourteen foot, ten inches wide, with a twelve-foot transom. She's extra-heavy—he goes offshore and doesn't let weather faze him too much. This one, I'd say, was the best I ever did as far as construction, but after I got it done, I told him, 'You'd better take care of it, 'cause you aren't gonna get me to do another one.' She's got inch-and-a-half planks—cedar, of course. I had to store all the cedar inside, and I had to push it over the boat or under the boat or drag it outside by the door and bring it around. I did it all myself and just about wore myself out. The timbers were so heavy, I put in two of them with chain falls. He's got a boat that'll hold him, I guarantee."

Willis calls over his shoulder to his wife, "What's the name of Killer's boat? Oh yes, the *April and Christy*. That's William Smith of West Jonesport—Killer, we call him. He's a real good fisherman. He's a relation to me—a cousin—but he's still a good fisherman. He's wore out I don't know how many crews; he works 'em hard. On his other boat, a forty-footer, he'd stay out there and work when some of those forty-five and fifty-footers would come in. He's taken chances—sometimes he didn't use sound reasoning, but he always survived."

Over the years, Willis built five boats for Earlon Beal and bought three of them back and fished them himself. The last one, which he called the *Elizabeth* after his daughter, he built in 1986. "This was a better boat than any of the others. Wider, higher, flatter, easier to see out of—a steadier boat. I really didn't think I could get a fiberglass boat that could work with her, but I have." Willis's present boat is the *Lucy W. Beal,* named for his mother. She is a fiberglass RP 35. He says about the boat, "I don't think there's a thing I would change.

"RP's 35 is like the boats I built in '85 and '86, with a higher, straighter sheer than the older ones. They wanted it a foot longer and a foot wider, eight inches higher in the sides, and concave in the bow, rather than just flat. I made them a half model, and it seemed to satisfy them.

"The high, straight sheer makes the boat deep enough that the engine'll go underneath the floor without raising the hatch cover. It brings the self-bailing scuppers out of the water, too. I've been dragging all winter, with a heavy drag, and the only time I see water in the scuppers is if I get caught, but it doesn't stay there. Quahogging's the same way. I could drag quahog all day long and never see water.

"I don't build any boats any more," says Willis. "My main income is from fishing now—quahog dragging and lobstering and, last winter, dragging scallops from the last of December until April. I like the new 35 real well. I got the hull in return for designing it, and I finished it off. It's the best boat I've had. Of course, the engine is part of the making of it." He chose a 370-horsepower Volvo diesel and says it suits the boat well.

Willis admits that the design of lobsterboats has changed. "They're still a nice looking boat, but they don't have the pretty curves they used to—more sheer, more flare, and tumblehome on the stern. To me, that's the way they're supposed to be, but it isn't feasible nowadays."

He was the final holdout building wooden boats on Beals. "The materials got so expensive, and the time involved . . . They can lay up a 'glass boat in sixteen days, and I couldn't even get the ribs and the keel done in that length of time."

"I'm one of the old guys," Willis admits. "I have a 1978 Lincoln Town Car with forty-eight thousand miles, and I wouldn't swap it for a new one." Willis says he doesn't need the computers and all the gadgets the new cars have. "I got the electric windows and power seats and plenty of ride, and it didn't cost me $30,000. And I think the car's beautiful—straight lines and a lot of chrome. It had thirty-nine thousand miles on it when I bought it three years ago. It has the original paint, two original tires on it. It's black, with a black interior—you don't see that very often. I don't like the looks of the new ones. And my wife says, 'You sell it, and I'll divorce you.'" They've been married thirty-two years.

I ask Willis about the two traditional torpedo-stern lobsterboats that some consider to be the crowning achievements of his long boatbuilding career. "That was really a joy I didn't expect to do. Never ever dreamed I would. I'd got done building one year and was working on some traps on the wharf. A couple of guys came along, and one of them was Bradford Bernardo. 'I'm told you build the best boats around,' he said. I told him, 'Well, I've built a few, and I try to do it right.' He said he'd like to have a torpedo-stern boat. He had a summer place out on Hardwood Island, on the western end of the Reach. His grandfather and father had been in the stone business out there, and his grandfather used to have a torpedo-stern boat."

Willis asked Bradford how big a boat he was interested in. At first, he wanted a twenty-eight-footer, but after talking with Willis a few times, he decided on a thirty-four-footer, like most of the originals. "He didn't realize how narrow they are," says Willis. "By the time he got an engine in a twenty-eight-footer, he wouldn't have had room for passengers or any cargo or anything. I made the boat eight feet wide, which is a couple of feet wider than they used to be. My father had one, and he said he could reach coaming to coaming."

Bernardo's boat is open—there's not even a spray hood—and it steers with a tiller stick like the original torpedoes. But it carries a 455 Chevy engine. "It goes real good and works real nice," says Willis. "We've raced it several Fourth of Julys. The best we had it going, they tell me, is thirty-seven miles per hour."

Willis can remember seeing a torpedo-sterned boat when he was growing up, but he never got a ride in one. He has some photos of these shapely boats, and he also has a model that Alvin Beal built for him. "That model is the only boat I ever had built for me," says Willis. "It's kind of interesting—that five-foot torpedo cost about the same money as the thirty-footer my grandfather had built back in 1934. I've got a receipt that shows he paid for it in full; it was a little over $600, and that's what I paid for my model—$600."

The second torpedo Willis built fishes from Port Clyde, with a good friend at the helm. "His boat is almost like the boats we did in the early '70s, except with the round stern," says Willis. "It's ten-and-a-half feet wide, has the trunk cabin and house like those boats, and the bulkhead's in the center, with the engine part in and part out. He's having a ball with it. He never ever went lobstering before. He had a farm in Vermont, but he moved to Port Clyde and decided he'd like to do a little lobstering through the summer."

Willis has built two torpedo-stern lobsterboats in recent years. This one has a beam of just eight feet.

Willis says he's imagined building and owning a torpedo, "just to play with, look at, give rides." He hasn't had his own but says, "Bernardo told me to use his, and people would come up to me with tears in their eyes because it looked exactly like one they had. I took my father in it one day. We had a nice sail one Sunday afternoon, through where we used to camp and fish. It was a beautiful afternoon, couldn't have been any better. We cruised around those islands—course, I let him steer.

"He said he thought he'd never have a chance to ride in one of those boats again. Later, we were in kind of a hurry to get back, and at the end of the Reach I pulled it back in the corner and let it go—he liked speed, and I like speed, and my grandfather liked speed. My father talked about that afternoon often."

The elder Beal died not too long afterward. "It was the winter after I built the second torpedo. The doctors wanted to test him for this and that, but he said, 'No, I'm not going to do it.' Then one day he went out and fed the birds and swept a little snow off, and he come in and just dropped. That's how he'd have wanted to go. I'd love to have him back, I miss him, but I wouldn't have him back to be sick."

Hardest for Willis after his father's death was working in the boatshop.

"He used to always be there in the shop, working on trap gear. He'd come in after the mail arrived, then he'd come back later in the afternoon. It just seemed you'd hear that door open, and there he'd be. It's been five years, and still I think of him an awful lot. Even lobstering, there's one place where we used to go—Bunkers Hole. When the tide was up, we could come in the inlet and go out the outlet. He'd say, 'Let's go up through Bunkers Hole and have our lunch in there.' It was awful, the first time I went through there without him. I cried just like a baby.

"Years before, after he stopped coming with me, he'd call me up on the radio three or four times a day. 'I s'pose you're in such-and-such a place,' he'd say, and often he'd be just about right. And then he'd say, 'I wish I was out there.' Some fishermen are like that—they never get over it. My father-in-law had to give it up for health reasons, and stopping almost killed him. And a real good friend of mine would jump right out of bed every morning when he heard those engines crack, then he'd say, 'What in the world am I up for? I don't even have a boat.'

Now fishing out of Port Clyde, the other Willis Beal torpedo-stern is wider and carries a full house.

"My uncle Almer, he loved to fish, but when he quit, I'd ask him, 'Don't you miss it?' and he'd say, 'Nope, I can see the boats come and go,' and that was enough. But he loved to get out and sail. He went one time with my brother Robert and said he'd pay for the gas, and they had a great sail. They burned twenty-five or thirty gallons, but Robert said, 'Don't worry about the gas; anytime you want to sail, you just say so.'

Though Willis, himself, hasn't started to slow down yet, he's nostalgic about the heyday of wooden-boat construction on Beals Island. "When I started building, there were thirteen shops here, and another four in Jonesport, all building wooden boats. Some worked year 'round, and others like me would knock off in the summer and go lobstering." Willis's shop is right at the end of the bridge. "When I was launching boats, the bridge would be lined up with cars just like it was race day, Fourth of July. And people would want to help me or anyone. If the shop didn't have a skidway, men would line up and hold the boat up.

"They'd move the boat a half a mile or more, on logs, right down the street. Traffic would turn and go the other way. When Alvin Beal built the boat for my father it was that way. The boat had to go down the road and over a marshy place, and they had men pulling it. You couldn't use a vehicle in that swampy area—we didn't have trailers or four-wheel drives then like we have today. And the men didn't expect to get paid anything; they just did it to help. People would kind of know when a boat was ready to launch—they'd keep an ear out, and when it was time, they'd all be there."

That's how it is on Beals, Willis says; if anyone needs anything, everyone's there to help.

MAC PETTEGROW
Reconciling the Lobsterboat's
Past and Future

ac Pettegrow, now of Southwest Harbor, comes from Jonesport originally. He grew up in a little house right beside the bridge to Beals, though the bridge wasn't there then. Mac remembers, "Freddy Lenfestey and Milton Beal were always at the house, and they'd draw chalk pictures of the bridge that was someday going to go across. Freddy'd always draw boats racing underneath it." Mac's mother was a Beal; like every one of the boatbuilders across the Reach, he descends from Manwaring Beal. Boats are in his blood.

He is now involved in two operations: Pettegrow Custom Boat Shop in Southwest Harbor and WesMac in Surry. At Pettegrow, he says, "We build anything. It's all custom—wood, fiberglass, anything. Most of our boats are cold-molded now—wood and epoxy. It's 90 percent pleasure boats." WesMac is a partnership with Steve Wessel. By far the largest share of their business is building commercial fishing boats, primarily finishing lobsterboat hulls from other manufacturers. About one in five goes to a lobsterman; the rest are set up for other fisheries, commercial diving, research, and carrying passengers.

Mac has had a lot of experience building lobsterboats. He fished as a young man, and he has clear ideas about which designs are best suited for various applications. He is also acutely aware of the ways external events affect boatbuilding trends. "For awhile," he says, "the market was moving toward fifty feet, but the chance to build a lot of forty-six to fifty-foot fishing boats died when they put in the Hague Line [the boundary between the offshore waters

155

of the United States and Canada]. We've fished there since the 1400s, but now we can't.

"That's driven the offshore boats inshore, and forty-two feet is about as big as it's going to get. That's a good multi-fishery size; you can do a lot with it. We have to wait and see what the oil spill did in Rhode Island—there have been a lot of big lobsterboats there, forty-six- and forty-eight-footers. They're not fishing behind any islands; you clear the point, and you're in open water. And those guys fish 2,500 to 3,000 traps.

"I'm not sure there will be a market for those bigger boats unless a new fishery comes along," says Mac. "If, all of a sudden, they're paying as much for sea cucumbers as they are for tuna, then it might happen. And the red crab industry is going to be interesting to watch. If that develops, the guys already offshore in eighty-foot boats will be set up, but the guys with the bigger lobsterboats—those forty-six- and forty-eight-footers—will try it.

During our visit, WesMac is finishing a forty-six-footer as a passenger boat for the Caribbean. "It's going to be loaded heavy," says Mac, "but they'd only like to go thirteen or fourteen knots, and they don't want to burn a lot of fuel. Fuel's expensive down there. We're putting in a 400-horsepower diesel, and she'll burn ten or twelve gallons per hour at fourteen knots with thirty-nine people aboard—that's not bad. The boat's very stable, comfortable, and doesn't get anybody nerved up." But, he explains, the same hull can be set up to fulfill an entirely different function.

"We finished a Newman 46 lobsterboat and delivered it to Boston on the fifteenth of February. We averaged twenty knots for the trip and used 226 gallons of fuel, running in three- to five-foot stuff all the way. We came in with two or two and a half tons of ice built up, but that boat was at fighting weight when we launched it. It performed beautifully.

"Under forty-two feet, it's difficult to build a pretty boat that's functionally correct for the industry. To keep the scale, you need forty-two feet. Less than that, and you run into all kinds of problems. You can't get a sheer on it that a man can see over, and the width overwhelms the length. You start compromising immediately.

"But if you build a standing shelter that's two inches higher than looks good, pretty soon you're carrying it all the way forward, and it's terrible. When I make a compromise, I have to walk away and cool down. Then I can come back and compromise on something else.

"I'm working on a Holland 32 picnic boat right now, and the owner wanted a head and a shower. 'Can you take a shower on your knees?' I asked him. Well, he has a shower. He can't stand up in it, but the boat looks the way it ought to. It's going to Miami, where it'll be the smallest boat in the marina.

"That's a real down east boat, the Holland 32," says Mac. "It's not the most comfortable boat to fish out of—it'll keep you wet all day and roll you to death. And boy, is it tender! You throw a lunch box on the bow, and down she goes. But that Holland is the prettiest boat today. It's the only true down east boat in production. It goes good, but it's got to be light as a feather to do it. We've kept the picnic boat light—all the bulkheads are honeycomb, for instance.

"Most of the good lobsterboats are designed to be lobsterboats, not 'we-can-build-anything-on-it-for-you' boats. Calvin Beal, for instance, doesn't bring pleasure into it at all. His designs are working platforms only.

"Spencer Lincoln has done different things for different people. He un derstands function—unlike most designers, he'll give up the artistic and let function take its course. So, he's answered everybody's needs. Dave McGraw [then owner of Flye Point Marine] wanted a pickup truck—a lobsterboat with a big, wide, cockpit that would go well—and Spencer's BHM 31 is a good, popular boat that was a good value at the time. But it's nearly impossible to make a pleasure boat out of this hull—it wants the engine way forward.

"The Duffy 35 is the most successful, best-looking of Spencer's designs. When he designed the high-sheer model, it was meant to be a pleasure boat. It's got the engine set down low. Usually that doesn't work very well, but Spencer hit it on the money. It goes easily, fairly fast. And it's a good lobsterboat.

"The Young Brothers' 33 is a great lobsterboat, terrific. It's very fast—much faster than the Duffy 35 with the same horsepower—but if you make it weigh 18,000 pounds, it's no good at all. That's because it's a skeg boat. As a working boat, the Duffy 35 might weigh ten or twelve thousand, the Young Brothers' a little lighter. But the Duffy can take the added weight of a pleasure boat.

"The Young brothers understand the concept, the function. They don't build too heavy or too light—they understand what the owner's going to do with the boat. At the working weight the boat comes out at, it does very well at any inshore fishery. The bottoms are very slick, and they go real nice and efficient. But once they go over that weight, like any skeg boat, they lose their efficiency.

"The guys who go sticking—harpooning tuna—still like the soft-bilged, narrow boats because they're quiet, and they can sneak up on a fish easily," Mac explains. "For chunking—where they grind up chum in the water to attract the tuna, then catch them with a rod and reel—they like the wider boats fine. They don't go fishing in hurricanes, anyway.

"As for sport-fishing boats, the charter guys wanted to cut their fuel bills and thought they'd try Maine lobsterboats. That's fine till you get to Hatteras, and you add a bait freezer and a generator and so on, and there's eight-foot seas following you in every day. A wide stern and a fine front end make a horrible stern-sea boat. The lobster fisherman doesn't care about a following sea that much, because he's home by the time it comes in."

Mac notes an interesting phenomenon. "There's a resurgence in functional, pretty wooden boats. Peter Kass is building a real functional boat that looks like what a lobsterboat ought to look like. He'll die poor—he can't make much money doing what he's doing. But he's having a good time, and that's important.

"The fiberglass thing has kind of run the gamut—when you talk to Peter and he's got two or three years work lined up, it tells you something. Most of his buyers are coming out of 'glass boats. A fiberglass boat is just alive with vibration all the time. For a guy who puts 3,000 hours on his engine every year, that's a lot of vibration. Coring the hull does cut a lot of it down; some people are afraid of it, but it's all a matter of workmanship. The technology is there to do it properly. A good boatbuilder is a good boatbuilder.

In his new forty-two footer, Mac retained the traditional sheer and flare but went to a V-bottom.

"They've built a lot of pleasure boats on the new lobsterboat hulls," says Mac, "but it's difficult now, because they're not beautiful. They do have more room than they used to, but for the same price you can go buy a Bertram or a Hatteras, and it'll do the job better. Someone will see a picture in *Yachting* or someplace, and the boat's going thirty. He'll come in wanting one just like it, only he wants a washer and a dryer and this and that. I tell him he can't do it. He says, 'Oh yes I can, and I'm going to.' I tell him he can't, and I write on the plans for him just how fast the boat is going to go." After that, notes Mac, "Everybody just says 'Yup' until you launch the boat, and they push the throttle down, and they're six knots shy of what they wanted." That kind of owner, he argues, would be better off with a deep-V hull and twin diesels to carry all his equipment and go fast to boot.

But the deep-V design isn't perfect, either. "A lot of those hulls don't stabilize till twenty knots," Mac explains. "But on a bad day in a bad situation, you're only doing twelve, and the deep-V is wallowing and twisting and dipping its head and doing all these bad things. That's where the lobsterboat shines. It has its place, and it won't go away until the lobster fishery closes. Then we'll build a lot of picnic boats. The traditional lobsterboat is the ideal picnic boat for this coast." But the traditional hull shape isn't right for everyone.

Mac continues, "I just designed two boats that are lobsterboats above the water and yachts below—they'll carry weight and still go twenty knots. The young lions want to go out there and just tear it up. Right now, though, there's nothing on the market to do that with, so they're overpowering boats trying to achieve this speed. There's a commercial market there, too—it isn't a big market, and it won't take long to fill it up, but there's a void. A lot of guys want to be fastest and have the biggest gang of traps in the bay.

"I have a 42 and a 46, both with a down east sheer, a spoon bow, and a brand new, hard-chine bottom to make them great sea boats, transition boats. They'll be fast, stable—we still have a deep skeg and a real fine entry and a lot of deadrise forward. But the hull is fairly flat aft—actually it's a warped bottom. They'll lug a lot of weight for a commercial guy or for a yachtsman who needs the washer and dryer.

"Every boat's a compromise," says Mac. "Nobody can build a perfect one, because nobody's got that much money." But he hopes his new design will answer some of the shortcomings of earlier models. The hard-chine concept, which involves putting a sharp "corner" where the sides of the boat meet the bottom, seems to have appeared in a lot of Maine builder's minds lately.

They're putting lifting rails on racing lobsterboats, creating an artificial hard chine, and Mac Pettegrow isn't the only one who plans to come out with a hard chine boat.

Is this to be the latest evolution in Maine lobsterboats?

EPILOGUE
A Detective Story

There's something special about lobsterboats, fishermen, islands—a connection that transcends changes in time, location, and ownership.

I discovered that firsthand because I've long admired a Jonesporter that works from Islesboro, the *Downhomer*, and I wanted to know who built her.

Gilbert and Wallace Leach now own the boat. Gilbert bought her from John Tani, who had moved ashore to a farm in Morrill. Gilbert said she was built on Beals in 1973, but he didn't know by whom.

I found John Tani by phone. He said he didn't remember who built the *Downhomer*. He bought her about fifteen years ago from a Bruce somebody-or-other who had stopped fishing and was running the fisherman's co-op on Swans Island. The boat had the same name then and was red, as she is today.

I had a several-years-old regional phone book that listed the Swans Island Fisherman's Co-op. A woman answered their phone, and although she had only been on Swans Island a year, she thought the Bruce I was looking for was Bruce Colbeth. "He's out by Beals somewhere now," she told me.

Through Directory Assistance, I found Bruce Colbeth, who thought maybe Clifford Alley had built the *Downhomer*, though he wasn't sure. He was interested to know she was still lobstering. Bruce had bought the boat from some fellow in Deer Isle, but he couldn't remember the name. I called Glenn Holland, hoping he would be able to tell me about someone over that way I could call.

Better than that, he knew the boat. (I should have asked him in the first place.) Glenn told me she was indeed built by Clifford Alley, for Philip Thompson of Deer Isle.

Again using my old phone book, I found Philip, and he said yes, Clifford Alley had built the *Downhomer* for him, but it was in 1971, not 1973. She was always red. "Persian Red, that was the name of the color paint," he told me. "She had a 455 Olds in her, not high compression, but the next one to it. That thing would go—she goes some easy."

"Did you race her?" I asked.

The **Downhomer** *with her trademark Persian Red hull and elongated trunk-cabin windows*

"No—they didn't have no races around here back then," said Philip. "Well, I did hook onto a lot of people, just goin' along, you know. There was one feller in a Boston Whaler with seventy-some horsepower. I left him settin' there like his motor'd quit. But I never had the occasion to race her, not really." Philip fished the *Downhomer* "prob'ly eight or nine years" and then went to a 'glass boat.

"Did she always have that unusual trunk cabin window?" I asked.

"Oh yes, I designed that window," said Philip. "I drew it out on a piece of paper how I wanted it, and Clifford built it like that. Then a pile of boats around here had it—they started makin' them that way. It's such a big window that after it was done, he made a dowel—square on each end, but round where you can see it—and put it in right in the middle of the window, for the strength. I 'magine it's still there." (It is, though I hadn't noticed it before he mentioned it.)

I asked if he'd had spray rails on her. "Oh yes, I put those on," said Philip. "Oak, about three-quarter-inch square they was. And she had haulin' strips on both sides, made with the same sheer's the boat." And that's just how *Downhomer* looks today.

Thanking Philip, I told him it was fun to hear more about a vessel I'd admired for so long, and he said he enjoyed talking about the old boat, too. "I have a picture of her in the bedroom, right on the shelf," he said.

There is, in fact, something special about lobsterboats, fishermen, islands. Everyone I called in this quest was welcoming and friendly, even if some of them couldn't give me the information I sought. It was a perfectly understandable quest to them all, to discover the pedigree of a particular boat, a good boat.

As noted from the start of this book, lobsterboats are worthy beings, honored by those who design, build, and fish them, by those who work them in other fields, by those who play in them—and by standers-by, who only see them at their jobs. Their people are worthy, too. It has been an honor for me to meet those I have met, and with their help, to begin to understand their boats.

A Non-Definitive Glossary
of Words as Used in this Book

aft—toward the stern (back) of the boat

athwartships—across the boat, from side to side

autopilot, Autohelm—a mechanism that steers the boat automatically

Avon—an inflatable rubber boat (brand name)

banding—putting rubber bands around lobster claws so they can't pinch

beam—the width of a vessel at its widest part

back down—move backward, under power or sail

bilge—1) the lowest part of the interior of a boat's hull; 2) the rounded portion of the hull where the sides of the boat meet the bottom. A soft bilge is gently rounded; a hard bilge has a tighter radius

bilge pumps, automatic and otherwise—pumps which remove water from the bilge

Billings—Billings Diesel and Marine Service, in Stonington

bright—finished with clear varnish (as opposed to paint)

built-down—constructed with the frames or hull bottom joining the keel in a plane nearly parallel with the sides of the keel, forming an S-curve from rail to keel (as opposed to skeg-built)

bulkhead—a partition running athwartships, providing support for the hull; on a lobsterboat the main bulkhead separates the standing shelter from the trunk cabin

cage—a steel structure installed over the propeller to preventing its fouling line and other debris

carrier, sardine—a boat used to carry fish, usually juvenile herring, from where they're caught to the shore-based processing plant

carvel—built with the external planks set edge to edge, smooth-surfaced (as opposed to lapstrake or strip-built)

catalyst—a chemical compound which, when mixed with resin, causes it to set up and harden

caulk (verb)—make plank seams watertight; formerly oakum and tar were used, but today polysulfide and silicone compounds are more common.

chopper gun—a hand-triggered device for applying a mixture of chopped fiberglass roving and resin at high speed during the layup of a hull

clam roller—a wooden basket used to carry clams

coaming—the raised edge around the cockpit; helps to keep water from coming in

Coast Guard license—a license to operate a commercial, passenger-carrying vessel

164

core (as in cored construction)—sheets of material such as balsa or foam incorporated into a fiberglass laminate to make the boat stiffer and/or lighter

deadrise—angle of the rise from the keel to the turn of bilge, i.e., the degree of V in the hull

deep-V—a bottom configuration in which steep deadrise (normally greater than twenty degrees) is carried the whole length of the hull

double-ender—a vessel whose bow and stern are both sharp

down cast cruiser—a pleasure boat based on a lobsterboat hull

fastenings—the screws, bolts or rivets that hold a boat together

fathom—six feet

flare—upward and outward curving of the sides at the bow; helps turn back spray

forefoot—the point at which the vertical portion of the bow joins the keel

freeboard—the distance from the rail to the water

gang—a series of lobster traps on a single line

garboard—the key plank in the area where the keel joins the bottom; or, in a fiberglass boat, that area itself

GPS—Global Positioning System, an electronic navigation system that uses satellites

handlining—fishing with a hand-held line and baited hooks

hard chine—a sharp angle between the side of the boat and the bottom

hatch—an opening in the deck, covered by a hatch cover

head boats—vessels that take paying customers sightseeing or fishing; each person pays so much "per head"

heading traps—replacing the knitted netting inside a lobster trap

house—a cabin above deck

keel—the longitudinal structure forming the backbone of a vessel and running the length of the bottom

knot—one nautical mile per hour—approximately 6,076 feet per hour

laminate—the layers that make up a fiberglass structure

lapstrake—constructed with the planks overlapping each other at the edges (as opposed to carvel)

layup (noun)—a thickness built up of fiberglass cloth, woven roving, and/or chopped-strand mat saturated with resin, or the process of creating same

left-handed boat—a vessel set up to haul traps from the left, or port, side (as opposed to a right-handed boat)

lobster car—a floating box in which caught lobsters are stored until they are sold

lobster smack—in earlier days, a larger vessel that transported substantial quantities of live lobsters to distant markets along the coast

lobster traps (sometimes called pots)—the traps set to catch lobsters; once wood, they are now usually vinyl-covered wire mesh

lobster yacht—another name for a down east cruiser, preferred by some

loft (verb)—to expand boat plans full size to use in construction

loran—an electronic navigation system based on land stations

make-and-break engine—an early, single-cylinder engine that had a unique, rhythmic sound due to peculiarities of ignition

mold—the "female" form in which fiberglass structures, including hulls, are laminated

nun—a red navigation buoy

one-lunger—a single-cylinder engine

pay—to caulk deck seams

peapod—a small, round bottomed, double-ended rowing boat

pegging (lobsters)—before banding became common, pegs were driven into the joint of lobsters' claws to prevent pinching

picnic boat—a pleasure boat, often open-topped, based on a lobsterboat hull; used primarily for day trips

planing—traveling fast enough for the hull to climb up onto its own bow wave

platform—the deck on which the fisherman works

plug—the "male" form over which a mold is created

ports—windows in the hull

pram—a small rowing boat with a square bow

purse seining—fishing in open waters with a net that surrounds the fish

rabbet line—a recess cut into in the face of a timber to receive planking, as on the keel and stem

rail—the reinforcing member installed along the line where the deck and hull join

resin—the viscous, polyester- or epoxy-based liquid that saturates the fabric in fiberglass layup

Revenue Cutter—a government patrol boat

rocker—longitudinal convex curvature in the hull bottom, running from the bow to the stern

rooster tail—a high arc of water kicked up (by the propeller) behind a fast power boat

rudder—an underwater vertical blade that is turned to steer the boat

run—the path the water takes going under a hull

see-clear spinner, Clearview—a device incorporating a rapidly spinning arm in a disk that is installed in a wheelhouse window; throws off rain or spray, making a clear spot

sheer, sheerline—the upward sweep of the rail from stern to bow

shoal—shallow water caused by an underlying rocky ledge or sandbar

shoal-draft boat—a vessel that can operate in minimal depths

skeg—an extension of the lower edge of the keel (supports the bottom end of the rudder post); *or,* an external keel applied to the bottom of a boat

skeg-built—constructed with the frames or hull bottom joining the keel in a plane nearly perpendicular to the sides of the keel (as opposed to *built-down*)

spray rails—longitudinal strips applied to or molded into a boat's hull to deflect water

steadying sail—a small sail on a short mast mounted aft to provide stability when a lobsterboat is hauling traps in choppy seas

stem—the foremost upright timber, into which the planks are rabbeted; also, the vertical, or near vertical, leading edge of the bow

stern—the rear part of the vessel

sternman—the second person, or helper, on a working lobsterboat

stern post—in a wooden boat, an upright timber forming the after end of the keel

stop seining—using netting to block the opening to a cove, trapping the fish therein

stringer—a longitudinal hull-strengthening member

strip planking—constructing a hull using more-or-less square strips of stock nailed and/or glued one atop the other

stuffing box—the sealed fitting by which the propeller shaft passes through the hull

surtax—a federal program (1990 to 1993) that placed a 10 percent surtax on various new luxury items, including pleasure boats valued at $100,000 or more

swing a smaller (or bigger) wheel—use a propeller of lesser (or greater) diameter

through-hull—a fitting that passes from the inside of the boat to the outside; commonly used where engine-cooling water enters

torpedo stern—an elliptical stern slanting upward and inboard from the waterline

transom—the portion of the hull's surface that runs athwartships at the stern

trunk cabin—a forward cabin topped by a low enclosed structure that projects above the deck

tumblehome—an inward curving of the sides at the stern, making the boat wider at the waterline than at the rail

urchins (also "green gold")—sea urchins, which are harvested by divers or by dragging; the roe is sold for high prices, primarily to Japanese markets

V-berth—the triangular forward berth in a vessel

V-bottom—a boat bottom that is angled, rather than rounded

V-drive—a gearbox that changes the direction of the shaft, allowing the engine to be mounted farther aft

washboard—the outer deck around the cockpit

Wayfarer—Wayfarer Marine Corporation, a large boatyard in Camden

wheel—1) propeller; 2) steering wheel

wineglass stern (or wineglass transom)—the after end of a built-down hull, where the sides and bottom join the keel in a curve similar to the sides and stem of a wineglass

wood borer—an insect, crustacean, or mollusk that bores into wood

wooding the hull—stripping a wooden boat of all old paint

woven roving—the heavy fabric used in fiberglass construction